**New Directions for Teaching and Learning**

Marilla D. Svinicki
EDITOR-IN-CHIEF

R. Eugene Rice
CONSULTING EDITOR

# Exploring Research-Based Teaching

Carolin Kreber

EDITOR

Number 107 • Fall 2006
Jossey-Bass
San Francisco

EXPLORING RESEARCH-BASED TEACHING
*Carolin Kreber* (ed.)
New Directions for Teaching and Learning, no. 107
*Marilla D. Svinicki*, Editor-in-Chief
*R. Eugene Rice*, Consulting Editor

Microfilm copies of issues and articles are available in 16mm and 35mm, as well as microfiche in 105mm, through University Microfilms, Inc., 300 North Zeeb Road, Ann Arbor, Michigan 48106-1346.

NEW DIRECTIONS FOR TEACHING AND LEARNING (ISSN 0271-0633, electronic ISSN 1536-0768) is part of The Jossey-Bass Higher and Adult Education Series and is published quarterly by Wiley Subscription Services, Inc., A Wiley Company, at Jossey-Bass, 989 Market Street, San Francisco, California 94103-1741. Periodicals postage paid at San Francisco, California, and at additional mailing offices. POSTMASTER: Send address changes to New Directions for Teaching and Learning, Jossey-Bass, 989 Market Street, San Francisco, California 94103-1741.

*New Directions for Teaching and Learning* is indexed in College Student Personnel Abstracts, Contents Pages in Education, and Current Index to Journals in Education (ERIC).

SUBSCRIPTIONS cost $80 for individuals and $195 for institutions, agencies, and libraries in the United States. Prices subject to change. See order form at end of book.

EDITORIAL CORRESPONDENCE should be sent to the editor-in-chief, Marilla D. Svinicki, Department of Educational Psychology, University of Texas at Austin, One University Station, D5800, Austin, TX 78712.

www.josseybass.com

# Contents

# FROM THE SERIES EDITOR

*About This Publication.* Since 1980, *New Directions for Teaching and Learning* (*NDTL*) has brought a unique blend of theory, research, and practice to leaders in postsecondary education. *NDTL* sourcebooks strive not only for solid substance but also for timeliness, compactness, and accessibility.

The series has four goals: to inform readers about current and future directions in teaching and learning in postsecondary education, to illuminate the context that shapes these new directions, to illustrate these new directions through examples from real settings, and to propose ways in which these new directions can be incorporated into still other settings.

This publication reflects the view that teaching deserves respect as a high form of scholarship. We believe that significant scholarship is conducted not only by researchers who report results of empirical investigations but also by practitioners who share disciplined reflections about teaching. Contributors to *NDTL* approach questions of teaching and learning as seriously as they approach substantive questions in their own disciplines, and they deal not only with pedagogical issues but also with the intellectual and social context in which these issues arise. Authors deal on the one hand with theory and research and on the other with practice, and they translate from research and theory to practice and back again.

*About This Volume.* There has been quite a push to base teaching on research findings in learning and development. Teachers are also encouraged to get involved in their own classroom research as part of the scholarship of teaching and learning. This issue addresses that impetus from several different perspectives within the academy.

Marilla D. Svinicki
Editor-in-Chief

MARILLA D. SVINICKI *is associate professor of educational psychology at the University of Texas at Austin.*

# EDITOR'S NOTES

The purpose of this volume is to illustrate the wide scope of possibilities in interpreting and promoting research-teaching synergies. This is achieved in Part One of the volume. At the same time it was a goal of this volume to look more explicitly at what institutions can do to promote two distinct forms of "research-based teaching." This is achieved in Parts Two and Three.

Part Two explores research-based teaching as student-focused, inquiry-based learning. Thus construed, students are not simply taught the discipline-based content knowledge that has been generated through research, nor are they simply taught the process of knowledge construction within the discipline or subject; instead, they themselves become generators of this knowledge.

Part Three espouses a very different conceptualization of "research-based teaching" by shifting the lens to those who are doing the teaching. According to this perspective, teaching that is research-based is teaching that is characterized by inquiry into the process of teaching itself.

The volume brings together a group of well-established scholars in the field of higher education to share and discuss their respective views on the relationships between teaching and research. Though other excellent recent publications exist that explore these links (for example, Brew, 2003; Elton, 2005; Jenkins and Healey, 2005), the present volume is distinctive in that it brings together an international group of colleagues from Canada, Australia, Britain, and the United States, each known for a specified body of work that in unique and significant ways contributes to the crucial question of how to support undergraduate students in their learning and the important role research-based teaching plays in this regard.

## Outline of Chapters That Follow

Each contributor to this volume was asked to delve into a different question. Part One of the volume consists of three chapters that explore various possibilities of promoting teaching-research synergies. In the first chapter I provide a general introduction to the volume and discuss why developing research-teaching synergies is becoming increasingly important. I also stress the need to conceptualize educational development within this context. In Chapter Two, Angela Brew addresses the question of how stronger teaching-research links could be built into the organization of departments and institutions by drawing on her extensive experience in generating such links at

NEW DIRECTIONS FOR TEACHING AND LEARNING, no. 107, Fall 2006  © Wiley Periodicals, Inc.
Published online in Wiley InterScience (www.interscience.wiley.com) • DOI: 10.1002/tl.238

the University of Sydney in New South Wales. In Chapter Three, Andrew Castley discusses how an academic practice unit wishing to promote closer research teaching links could support academic staff and postgraduate students in their professional development.

Part Two explores research-based teaching from a particular vantage point, namely, construed as teaching that is characterized by students' direct engagement in inquiry-based learning. It consists of three chapters. In Chapter Four, Lewis Elton analyzes the nature of effective or exemplary teaching in a learning environment that promotes close research and teaching links and explores specifically the pedagogical significance of problem-based learning. In Chapter Five, Mick Healey and Alan Jenkins discuss how stronger teaching and research links could be built into undergraduate courses and programs and provide many useful examples and suggestions. Heather Kanuka, in Chapter Six, offers her insights into some of the challenges and opportunities posed by information communication technologies in promoting inquiry-based student learning, focusing in particular on the role of the Web.

In Part Three, the focus shifts from the learner to the teacher, in that research-based teaching is interpreted as teaching informed by, or based on, pedagogical inquiry. In consists of four chapters. In Chapter Seven, Mary Huber links the notion of inquiry-based learning about teaching explicitly to the scholarship of teaching and learning and explores how the disciplines can uniquely contribute to and benefit from such work. In Chapter Eight, I offer some suggestions for how educational development units, or faculty development units as they are sometimes called, could promote the process of inquiry-based learning about teaching, emphasizing the importance of fostering critical reflection on present knowledge and practices. In Chapter Nine, Vaneeta-marie D'Andrea discusses the challenges associated with carrying out such work and explores in particular different methodological approaches that can be taken in inquiry-based learning about teaching. David Gosling, in Chapter Ten, considers the important question of whether, and if so how, an inquiry-based or evidence-based approach to teaching and educational development would enhance practice. Finally, in Chapter Eleven, I discuss some of the themes emerging from the previous chapters.

Carolin Kreber
Editor

## References

Brew, A. "Teaching and Research: New Relationships and Their Implications for Inquiry-Based Teaching and Learning in Higher Education." *Higher Education Research and Development*, 2003, 22(1), 3–18.

Elton, L. "Scholarship and the Research and Teaching Nexus." In R. Barnett (ed.), *Reshaping the University: New Relationships Between Research, Scholarship and Teaching.* Maidenhead, U.K.: Open University Press, 2005.

Jenkins, A., and Healey, M. *Institutional Strategies to Link Teaching and Research.* York, U.K.: Higher Education Academy, 2005. http://www.heacademy.ac.uk/resources.asp?process=full_recordandsection=genericandid=585. Accessed Dec. 2005.

CAROLIN KREBER *is director of the Centre for Teaching, Learning and Assessment at the University of Edinburgh, where she is also professor of teaching and learning in higher education in the Department of Higher and Community Education.*

# PART ONE

# Exploring Different Possibilities in Promoting Teaching-Research Synergies

# 1

*Research-based teaching is becoming increasingly impor-*
*tant as the mandate of higher education institutions is*
*being broadened.*

# Introduction: The Scope of Possibility in Interpreting and Promoting Research-Based Teaching

*Carolin Kreber*

In this first chapter I provide the background to the volume and explore the question of why establishing stronger teaching and research synergies is becoming increasingly important. I also suggest that there is a need to better understand the practice of educational development within this context.

## Some Challenges Associated with University Teaching

University teaching today is more complex than in the past. The move from elite to mass higher education (to almost universal access) in most industrialized nations meant that classes not only got bigger but also far more diverse. Undergraduates today no longer can be assumed to be full-time students, predominantly male, enter higher education right after high school, complete their degree at the institution where they started out, have English as their first language, or share the same cultural and socioeconomic heritage. Most universities have also incorporated into their widening participation agenda policies that allow improved access to students with special needs, including learning disabilities. There is some evidence that students today are more tolerant and encouraging of diversity with respect to ethnic background and lifestyle issues (Stark and Lattuca, 1997). But that is not all that is different today.

NEW DIRECTIONS FOR TEACHING AND LEARNING, no. 107, Fall 2006    © Wiley Periodicals, Inc.
Published online in Wiley InterScience (www.interscience.wiley.com) • DOI: 10.1002/tl.239

Research exploring changes in the educational aspirations of students since the mid-1960s indicates that their goals have become progressively more vocational (Dey, Astin, and Korn, 1991; Gilbert and others, 1997; Levine and Cureton, 1998; Sax, Astin, Korn, and Mahoney, 1999). This finding may not be surprising, as lower levels of government funding have led many universities (in jurisdictions where the option exists) to set their own tuition fees. In the province of Alberta in Canada, for example, tuition for a regular undergraduate program has risen more than 100 percent over the last ten-year period (AUCC, 2005), and it is not uncommon for students to be $20,000 (CDN) in debt by the time they have earned their degree. Since many students work, at least part-time, to pay for their tuition, it also takes them longer to complete their studies, which in turn raises their debt. Rising tuition fees also mean that students have become more vocal with regards to what they believe the university ought to offer them; the degree, particularly one with good standing, they perceive more and more as the key (and an imperative) for future economic and professional prosperity. As a consequence grades tend to matter much more to them than in the past. And who is to blame students for not entering higher education exclusively for the sake of learning if there is a strong perception that middle-class jobs increasingly require a first degree and many require a postgraduate degree?

In addition, universities are increasingly expected to do more with less. Despite fewer resources, universities are asked to broaden their mandate rather than to limit it to what they do best (though doing the latter is certainly not an uncommon suggestion made by representatives of elite institutions). Next to preparing students academically, governments, industry, and the public at large count on universities to prepare students also for their civic, personal, and professional roles in later life. While the importance of these goals cannot be denied, the requirement raises the question of whether academics are adequately prepared for such a complex undertaking. Years of study to obtain a postgraduate degree within their chosen field of specialization surely prepared them well for a career as researchers, but given today's complex higher education environment and the diversity and multiple aspirations and needs of students, it is questionable whether disciplinary content and research expertise provide a sufficiently sound basis for effectively facilitating learning and student development. As the institutions' teaching mandate was broadened, pressures on faculty to be active in research also increased. In some countries, for example the United Kingdom, the external cyclical assessment of a department's research quality is directly linked to funding (the so-called Research Assessment Exercise), and despite intensified performance accountability with respect to teaching, faculty's research productivity is still the main criterion in hiring and promotion decisions at universities in most countries.

To complicate matters further, this decade has begun to witness the retirement of a large proportion of the professoriate who assumed tenured positions during a time of massive expansion and the sheer unlimited flow of resources characterizing the sector until the mid-1970s. In the early

NEW DIRECTIONS FOR TEACHING AND LEARNING • DOI: 10.1002/tl

twenty-first century, few of the resulting openings will be re-advertised as tenure-track positions, and already much undergraduate teaching is being carried out by postgraduate students, along with part-time and contract faculty. To what extent, one may ask, are they prepared for their roles, and what form should such preparation take?

## Establishing Stronger Teaching and Research Synergies

As Angela Brew suggests in Chapter Two, the relationship between teaching and research is understood differently by different people depending, among other factors, on the conceptions of research and of teaching they hold. The purpose of this introductory chapter is not to discuss the multiple ways in which the relationship can be conceptualized and the implications of these conceptualizations for how teaching or departments are organized, but to explore more specifically the question of why the research-teaching nexus should concern us at all.

Several authors suggest that the challenges of the twenty-first century require higher education institutions to prepare students as independent thinkers, productive citizens, and future leaders (Baxter Magolda, Terenzini, and Hutchings, n.d.). The Association of American Colleges and Universities argued in *Greater Expectations,* a widely cited United States National Panel Report (2002), that in order to be successful in an increasingly complex world, undergraduate students need to experience a solid liberal education. Specifically, the report advises that students need to develop mastery of intellectual and practical skills, knowledge about forms of inquiry underlying natural and social science disciplines, and responsibility for their personal actions as well as civic values. The latter point in particular is also being emphasized by a Carnegie Foundation report on the purposes of undergraduate education in the United States (Colby, Ehrlich, Beaumont, and Stephens, 2003). In Canada, Axelrod (2002) cautioned that political and economic pressures are determining more and more how the purposes of higher education are being defined in that country and argued strongly for the importance of not losing sight of the essential role of the liberal arts in Canadian undergraduate education and that their objectives (such as to cultivate intellectual creativity, autonomy, and resilience) should be integrated into scientific, technical, and professional education.

The United Kingdom government (DfES, 2003), like that of most nations, recently highlighted higher education's important role in fostering personal and intellectual fulfillment of individuals as well as the economic and social well-being of the nation and emphasized that in an increasingly competitive world "the role of higher education in equipping the labour force with appropriate and relevant skills" is a central goal (p. 10). One of the major aims of higher education in the United Kingdom, therefore, is seen in the employability of graduates (Yorke and Knight, 2003). Yet, U.K.-based

NEW DIRECTIONS FOR TEACHING AND LEARNING • DOI: 10.1002/tl

scholar Barnett (2000) has argued that students need to be prepared not only for a world characterized increasingly by "performativity" but also for the multiple challenges posed by a world of "supercomplexity." A supercomplex world is one where the frameworks by which we orient ourselves no longer remain uncontested but are instead being challenged and require reconstructing. Most important to this present discussion, the skills, abilities, and personal qualities typically associated with employability, such as self-management, critical analysis, creativity, ethical sensitivity, the capacity to act morally, solve problems, resolve conflict, make decisions, negotiate, work in teams, and work cross-culturally, to mention but a few (Yorke and Knight, 2003), are critical not only for being successful in the work setting but also for dealing with "supercomplexity."

It is probably fair to say that countries around the world recognize that higher education institutions need to respond thoughtfully to the new and more complex political, economic, and social-cultural contexts of our times (see also UNESCO WCHE, 1998). It is perhaps also fair to suggest that the classic conception of the teaching-research relationship, whereby teaching is led by research and usually characterized by a teacher-focused transmission approach, if put into practice by itself, has been found wanting in its potential to respond adequately to these larger issues and to develop in undergraduate students the thinking skills they need to be prepared for later life. What is perhaps less clear is what alternative form the response should take. However, suggestions have been offered.

For example, Baxter Magolda (1999) argues that students need to develop a certain intellectual (and intra- and inter-personal) maturity to deal adequately with the various challenges of our times and suggests that higher education pedagogies should be designed such that they promote what she calls student "self-authorship." Another prominent theme in the higher education teaching and learning literature is a concern with developing higher-order thinking skills (Donald, 2002). Both authors suggest that students need to learn the thinking processes associated with solving complex problems and constructing new knowledge in their discipline. Similar arguments are made by proponents of service learning (Ehrlich, 2001; Lempert, 1996; Rhoads and Howard, 1998) who emphasize the need for students to be involved in problem-based and collaborative learning and the solving of real problems. They add the dimension of moral development and argue that students develop not only intellectually but also morally as they interact with communities different from their own.

Based on extensive interviews over several years with undergraduate students from different disciplines, Baxter Magolda (1992, 1999) offered three principles of a "constructive-developmental pedagogy" that would support students in this process of gaining intellectual (and personal) maturity: to validate students as knowers, to situate learning in the students' experience, and to conceive of learning as mutually constructing knowledge. Evidently, such an approach to higher education pedagogy would be focused on the learners (rather than on the teacher) and would involve them directly in the process of knowledge construction through inquiry-based learning (see also Healey and Jenkins in Chapter Five of this volume). Student-focused, inquiry-based learning has been identified as a promising pedagogical approach to preparing students for the challenges associated with their future personal, professional, and civic lives. Involving students in research-like activities to support their learning, therefore, is not only a possible way of creating research-teaching synergies but one that is particularly meaningful and important given the challenges of our times.

## The Practice of Educational Development

Part Three of this volume explores research-based teaching as inquiry-based learning about teaching. This perspective, although at times overlooked when research-teaching links are discussed, is as important as the previous one. The argument is straightforward: In order to best support students in their learning, faculty (and others with teaching responsibilities in our colleges and universities) need to acquire a deeper understanding of the processes of teaching and learning themselves. The entire idea of changing higher education curricula so that they better prepare students for the ever more complex dimensions of work, society, and life poses considerable challenges for institutions. To what extent, one may ask, are faculty, or entire departments, prepared for designing curricula and courses that are suitable for promoting in students the abilities, skills, and personal attributes required to navigate effectively within the complexities of today's world? Moreover, to what extent are they prepared for designing curricula and courses that would specifically involve students in inquiry-based learning? And to what extent are the approaches that eventually get chosen meaningful or effective with an increasingly diverse student population? It is argued in this volume that an important aspect of research-based teaching is to have teaching itself be informed by what is known and what becomes known about teaching and learning through existing and ongoing pedagogical research. This pedagogical research is comprised, on the one hand, by the inquiries teachers may carry out themselves into their own teaching and their students' learning, and on the other hand, by the ever-growing, discipline-specific and generic literature on teaching and learning reporting on research conducted by others. An educational development unit wishing to optimize the student learning experience on campus may wish not only to "tell" departments and faculty about what we now know about "effective pedagogy" (and student-focused, inquiry-based learning) but also involve staff directly in exploring how best to facilitate such learning of their students within their unique disciplinary and departmental contexts. And as Mary Huber argues so eloquently in Chapter Seven in this volume, as a result of this inquiry-based learning about teaching, the disciplines themselves may benefit as well.

## References

Association of American Colleges and Universities. *Greater Expectations: A New Vision for Learning as a Nation Goes to College.* Washington, D.C.: Association of American Colleges and Universities, 2002.

AUCC. *Canadian Universities, University of Alberta, Enrollment and fees.* 2005. http://www.aucc.ca/can_uni/our_universities/alberta_e.html. Accessed Aug. 2, 2006.

Axelrod, P. D. *Values in Conflict: The University, the Marketplace and the Trials of Liberal Education.* Montréal, Quebec: McGill-Queen's University Press, 2002.

Barnett, R. "Supercomplexity and the Curriculum." *Studies in Higher Education,* 2000, 25(3), 255–265.

Baxter Magolda, M. *Knowing and Reasoning in College: Gender-Related Pattern in Students' Intellectual Development.* San Francisco: Jossey-Bass, 1992.

Baxter Magolda, M. *Creating Contexts for Learning and Self-Authorship: Constructive-Developmental Pedagogy.* Nashville, Tenn.: Vanderbilt University Press, 1999.

Baxter Magolda, M. and Terenzini, P. T., with Hutchings, P. "Learning and Teaching in the 21st Century: Trends and Implications for Practice." In C. S. Johnson and H. E. Cheatham (eds.), *Higher Education Trends for the Next Century: A Research Agenda for Student Success.* Washington, D.C.: American College Personnel Association, n.d. [1999]. http://www.acpa.nche.edu/seniorscholars/trends/trends4.htm. Accessed May 2000.

Colby, A., Ehrlich, T., Beaumont, E., and Stephens, J. *Educating Citizens: Preparing America's Undergraduates for Lives of Moral and Civic Responsibility.* San Francisco: Jossey-Bass, 2003.

Dey, E. L., Astin, A. W., and Korn, W. S. *The American Freshman: Twenty-Five Year Trends, 1966–1990.* Los Angeles: UCLA Higher Education Research Institute, 1991.

DfES (Department for Education and Skills). "The Future of Higher Education." Unpublished paper. Norwich, United Kingdom, 2003.

Donald, J. G. *Learning to Think: Disciplinary Perspectives.* San Francisco: Jossey-Bass, 2002.

Ehrlich, T. "Education for Responsible Citizenship: A Challenge for Faculty Developers." In D. Lieberman and C. Wehlburg (eds.), *To Improve the Academy: Resources for Faculty, Instructional, and Organizational Development.* Bolton, Mass.: Anker, 2001.

Gilbert, S., and others. *From Best Intentions to Best Practices: The First Experience in Canadian Post-Secondary Education.* Columbia: University of South Carolina, 1997.

Lempert, D. H. *Escape from the Ivory Tower: Student Adventures in Democratic Experiential Education.* San Francisco: Jossey-Bass, 1996.

Levine, A., and Cureton, J. S. *When Hope and Fear Collide: A Portrait of Today's College Students.* San Francisco: Jossey-Bass, 1998.

Rhoads, R. A., and Howard, J.P.F. (eds.). *Academic Service Learning: A Pedagogy of Action and Reflection.* San Francisco: Jossey-Bass, 1998.

Sax, L. J., Astin, A. W., Korn, W. S., and Mahoney, K. M. *The American Freshman: National Norms for Fall, 1998.* Los Angeles: Higher Education Research Institute, 1999.

Stark, J. S., and Lattuca, L. R. *Shaping the College Curriculum: Academic Plans in Action.* Needham Heights, Mass.: Allyn and Bacon, 1997.

UNESCO WCHE (World Conference on Higher Education). *Higher Education in the Twenty-First Century: Vision and Action.* Volume I: *Final Report.* Paris: UNESCO, 1998.

Yorke, M., and Knight, P. *The Undergraduate Curriculum and Employability.* York, U.K.: Higher Education Academy, 2003. http://www.heacademy.ac.uk/resources.asp?process=full_record&section=generic&id=248. Accessed July 2, 2006.

*CAROLIN KREBER is director of the Centre for Teaching, Learning and Assessment at the University of Edinburgh, where she is also professor of teaching and learning in higher education in the Department of Higher and Community Education.*

**2**

*When implementing institutional strategies to bring research and teaching together, learning occurs. A research-intensive university in Australia put in place institutional strategies to strengthen the relationship between research and teaching.*

# Learning to Develop the Relationship Between Research and Teaching at an Institutional Level

*Angela Brew*

Developing the relationship between teaching and research goes to the very heart of academic work. In each university people have varied ideas about how research links with teaching. They also have varying experiences and understandings of the nature of research, different approaches to teaching, and different ideas about how and whether to bring research and teaching together (Brew, 2003). Superficially, attempts to bring research and teaching together may result simply in using different language to describe existing practice or in faculty making more attempts to talk about their research in lectures. However, in looking more closely at what is involved in integrating research and teaching, substantial questions about the roles and responsibilities of universities arise. The nature of academic work undergoes reexamination. Questions are raised about what disciplinary knowledge is being developed and who is assumed to develop it. How faculty and students relate to each other and how university spaces are arranged and used also become subjects of discussion and debate. Indeed, the very purposes of higher education are called into question.

In order to discuss some general issues concerning possibilities for creating research and teaching synergies at an institutional level, this chapter focuses on my experience at the University of Sydney, a major, publicly funded research university in Australia. The complexity of a large and diverse institution means that attempts to change practice present many

NEW DIRECTIONS FOR TEACHING AND LEARNING, no. 107, Fall 2006 © Wiley Periodicals, Inc.
Published online in Wiley InterScience (www.interscience.wiley.com) • DOI: 10.1002/tl.240

challenges. Experience shows that it is important to ensure that policies and strategies to develop the relationship between teaching and research do not result in change only at the superficial levels, but can accommodate and encourage people to ask and discuss more substantial questions.

## Setting the Context

Institutional strategies and policies necessarily presuppose and also encourage particular views of the nature of academic work and the kind of relationships between faculty and students that are possible and appropriate. At the University of Sydney, initiatives to integrate research and teaching had as their starting point relevant aspects of the university's strategic plan:

- To provide curricula informed by current research, scholarship, creative works and professional practice
- To develop and reward well-qualified staff with a strong commitment to teaching informed by research and offer opportunities for teaching development
- To assist the transition of students into research-based programs through opportunities provided within undergraduate programs
- To support the conduct of outstanding research by both students and staff (University of Sydney, 2005).

These objectives provided the basis for a university-wide project to be established with two aims:

1. Increasingly employ undergraduate teaching and learning strategies that enhance the links between research and teaching and use scholarly inquiry as an organizing principle in departmental organization and curriculum development.
2. Encourage and reward the scholarship of teaching.

Undoubtedly, a strong climate of teaching development driven by a performance-based, funding-for-teaching system was a facilitative context for the development of research-teaching linkages. The funding system included the allocation of 0.5 percent of the university's teaching budget, according to what is known as the Scholarship Index. This measure rewards departments for scholarly activity related to teaching and learning according to a set of weighted criteria: a qualification in university teaching (10 points), a national teaching award (finalist) (5 points), a publication on university teaching (refereed article) (2 points), and so on.

It was in this context that a working group was established consisting of senior representatives from all seventeen faculties and charged with developing the integration of research and teaching at faculty, school, and departmental levels. This working group has been crucial to the success of the project thus far. The working group has established and audited the university according to a set of performance indicators to measure research-led teaching and the scholarship of teaching and learning. Other strategies include a Web site with a database of examples of research-led teaching and learning and the scholarship of teaching and learning, various steps taken to explore students' perceptions of research in the university, university-wide showcases of scholarly practice in learning and teaching, and workshops and forums organized in many faculties. In addition, reviews of faculties carried out by the Academic Board (the main academic decision-making body of the university) required evidence of the extent of research-led teaching and learning.

Five years from the commencement of the project, these strategies have been reflected in new policies, for example in a University of Sydney policy statement of what is understood by research-led teaching and the scholarship of teaching and a renewed commitment to research-led teaching in a new strategic plan: "A distinctive feature of study at the University of Sydney is its insistence on research-led teaching, both in content and delivery" (University of Sydney, 2005).

## Performance Indicators for Research-Led Teaching and the Scholarship of Teaching and Learning

One important question when wanting to develop the relationship between teaching and research is how to tell that progress has been made. The working group, encouraged by the work of Hattie (2001), set about establishing performance indicators for research-led teaching and the scholarship of teaching.

Developing the indicators turned out to be an important process for working group members, as they came to understand what research-led teaching and the scholarship of teaching and learning could mean. Learning resulted from sharing ideas across the faculties and eventually agreeing on a set of twenty-seven indicators on seven key criteria:

1. Student awareness of and active engagement with research (including working as a consultant, performances, creative works, exhibitions, industrial and professional short-term placements, and clinical practice)
2. Academic staff capacity to integrate research and teaching (that is, all strategies used across the university to engage students in learning: lectures, tutorials, flexible, online and distance modes, clinical and bedside teaching, one-to-one and studio teaching, and so on)
3. Curriculum designed to engage students in a variety of research-based activities, induct them into the research community, and develop their awareness of research
4. Departmental encouragement for aligning research and teaching
5. Faculty support and encouragement for strengthening the nexus between research and teaching

6. College recognition and support for the development of the links between research and teaching (faculties are grouped into three "colleges")
7. University commitment to the development of strong relationships between teaching and research

Once the indicators were established, the working group set about collecting data on them; this proved to be a very effective strategy for getting faculty in schools and departments talking about what was meant by research-led teaching. In the course of this work, a great deal was learned about what is meant by research-led teaching and the scholarship of teaching and learning and about what is needed to develop it.

## Student Awareness of Research

Some indicators were designed to capture students' awareness of research. These indicators stemmed from the view that research-led teaching had to be seen as much from the students' perspectives as from the perspectives of faculty. It was considered that claims that teaching is research-led were not going to be credible if students had negative or no ideas about the university as a research environment, nor of the relationship between what they were learning and research.

To find out students' perceptions of the university as a research-intensive institution, the working group collaborated with the marketing department to obtain data on the views of incoming students, and a pilot study of students' experiences at the University of Sydney was carried out. This study confirmed the findings of Jenkins, Blackman, Lindsay, and Paton-Saltzberg (1998) and Zamorski (2002) that students are frequently unaware of the research of the university. In the future, students' perceptions are going to be monitored through new questions on a survey that is routinely sent to a random stratified sample of students each year. It will thus be possible to monitor changes in perceptions over time.

To realize that undergraduates had little idea of the university as a research institution was quite shocking to working group members; some strategies were consequently put in place to develop students' awareness of research.

## Academic Capacity to Integrate Research and Teaching

Successful integration of research and teaching is dependent upon strategies that take account of varying views of research, teaching, and knowledge, and the nature of scholarship within particular disciplinary areas. It is also dependent upon a variety of views of the nature of research-led teaching, research-based learning, or whatever terms are being used. Many of these ideas are taken for granted and tend not to be talked about unless they are seen as problematic, as, for example, they are in some new disci-

NEW DIRECTIONS FOR TEACHING AND LEARNING • DOI: 10.1002/tl

plinary areas. Changing people's views of the possibilities and practicalities of integrating research and teaching is perhaps the most challenging aspect of strategies to bring them together. Although the integration of research and teaching can be helped along by institutional measures that encourage and reward research-led teaching and the scholarship of teaching and learning initiatives, ultimately it is the perceptions of faculty and ways of thinking and acting that need to change. To bring about long-term and lasting changes requires time and patience. There is research evidence that extended discussion of the relationship is productive of changed ideas about what is possible and desirable. Jenkins and Zetter (2003), for example, report that a group of faculty from different institutions who met regularly over a two-year period to consider how to integrate research, teaching, and consultancy within the built environment disciplines developed sophisticated understandings of the possibilities through the process of dialogue.

Any attempts to bring research and teaching together need to take account of the ways in which academic work is changing. However, there is now an increasing number of new roles, including teaching-only positions (not hitherto commonplace in, for example, the United Kingdom and Australia), administrators with research functions, and many instructional and Web design roles. There is also an increase in sessional teachers. These roles are having a variety of effects on a university's capacity to integrate research and teaching. In performance and artistic areas, hiring casual teaching staff enables leading performers to be involved in teaching. However, in traditional subjects such as humanities, social sciences, and science, usually sessional teachers are neither leading practitioners nor researchers, which affects the capacity and willingness of faculty to integrate research and teaching. Other aspects of the way academic roles and responsibilities are changing that affect the university's capacity to integrate research and teaching include changes to tenure, the difficulty of gaining promotion without a substantial research record, the hiring of senior professional people without a track record in research, and the increasing difficulty for those in high-level university management positions to maintain a research profile. In addition, there is a growing trend for senior researchers in possession of research grants to "buy themselves out" of teaching (Brew, 2006).

While these changes in academic roles affect the steps a university needs to take in order to integrate research and teaching, it is not a necessary consequence of such positions that the gap between research and teaching should be widened. The University of Sydney working group found that more needs to be known about the effects of these changes. Some creative thinking about how to integrate research and teaching in ways that take account of these changes is required. This may mean, for example, integrating graduate research education and teaching development by involving graduate students in sharing their research with undergraduates as tutors. Casual or sessional staff, and indeed general staff, may be involved in supporting inquiry-based, problem-based curricula, and key researchers can be involved as keynote speakers in student research conferences and the like.

New kinds of positions need to be welcomed as providing opportunities to think creatively about relationships between different categories of staff within universities (Brew, 2006). Once perceptions begin to shift to thinking of all as being engaged in some form of learning through scholarly inquiry, faculty, students, and general staff all come to participate in a more inclusive scholarly learning community where each person's contribution is valued.

Hotly debated questions at the University of Sydney were whether a university's capacity to integrate research and teaching is dependent on teaching staff being research-active, however "research active" is defined (see Zetter, 2002), and whether senior faculty and key researchers need to be involved in teaching first- and second-year students. It is now considered important to increase students' awareness of and chances to participate in research in the first and second years, and it should be the case that in an environment where teachers are leading the research field, student learning should be more up to date than where teachers are not so engaged. However, in the absence of research evidence, there is by no means a clear view as to the effects of research on students' learning experiences or whether it results in better or more research-based education. Indeed, in my travels and discussions in numerous universities and in asking faculty to share examples of what they understand by research-led teaching, I have found that some of the most inventive examples are not confined to research universities. Students are capable of having a research-enhanced experience whether or not their teachers are active researchers. For example, Dwyer (2001) reports on a situation where small groups of students interview a researcher about his or her research. Different groups are allocated to different researchers. The teacher with responsibility for the class does not have to be a researcher.

## Engaging Students in Research-Based Activities and Curricula

Taking a traditional stance, there are a number of teaching activities in universities that mirror research activities. Essays, for example, which are perhaps the most common assessment method in the humanities and social sciences, require students to engage in research processes and scholarly work. Laboratory work and report writing common in the sciences and engineering also have their roots in research practice, as does field work in areas such as geography and environmental sciences. Nevertheless, a typical response to a policy of developing research-enhanced teaching and learning, including from working group members, is to redefine existing practice in research-led terms, that is, to simply change the language used to talk about such practices. This process is often the first step in developing a research-based curriculum. Yet the research on students' perceptions demonstrates that they are frequently unaware of these linkages with research. Changing traditional attitudes toward thinking about how one could link research and teaching more effectively has been a key challenge.

Such practices are more often than not implemented within a model of the relationship between research and teaching that sees research as the generation of what Gibbons and others (1994) call "Mode 1 knowledge" by a community of scholars separated from society and from teaching. In this model, teaching tends to be approached in what Prosser and Trigwell (1999) call a teacher-focused, information-transmission way, where the focus is on the teacher and what they desire and do with an intention to transfer pre-existing disciplinary knowledge to the student (Brew, 2003).

Within such a framework, the development of a research-based curriculum is considered to be a matter of ensuring that lectures are up to date, include the latest research findings, or contain anecdotal material about the process of discovery. The very fact that students have direct contact with active researchers, some of whom are leading experts in the field, is assumed to be a research-based experience. These ideas limit possibilities for action, but they may well be the starting point for development. A key issue is how to move practice to more student-focused approaches where students engage in research-based activities and research is viewed in what Gibbons and others (1994) term "Mode 2," that is, generating knowledge through a process of communication and negotiation integral with society.

The University of Sydney working group was confronted with a wide spectrum of different curriculum strategies ranging from teacher-focused information-transmission strategies to a range of student-focused strategies. In some of these strategies, students are involved in research "tasters," carrying out research for assignments or projects. In other examples more full-scale inquiries are conducted by students. More often than not, however, undergraduate students are kept at arms' length from the research effort of the department and carry out research-like activities alone or in groups of collaborating students. Some of the best examples of undergraduate students engaging in inquiry processes in order to learn come from professional areas. As professions become increasingly evidence based, valuing the use of research as an integral part of professional practice, students are also increasingly being required to engage in inquiring into aspects of practice in order to learn. However, even where the curriculum mirrors research practices, as in the case of problem- or inquiry-based learning, undergraduates tend to work in a domain that is separated from and often does not link to the research activities of their teachers. Exceptions to this situation are undergraduate research schemes where students are employed to work with individual academics or a research team during a summer recess. Such schemes are common in North America but with a few notable exceptions, are uncommon elsewhere.

I have found that it is in the sharing of examples that changes in perceptions begin to take place and myths are challenged. Doing this sharing is important because myths are often more obstructive than institutional structures. For example, if faculty believe that elaborate ethical-committee procedures are required before research-based learning practices can be implemented, they are unlikely to attempt to change. If they believe that students at the early stages of a degree are incapable of carrying out research, then they will limit research opportunities to the senior years. If they believe that research-based activities are not possible in the large classes they teach, they are unlikely to move to student-focused approaches to research-led teaching and learning. Holding up examples in cognate areas where students at different levels and in varying student cohorts engage in research-based learning challenges myths and beliefs and opens up possibilities for change.

## Departmental and Faculty Initiatives

A key feature of any institutional strategy to integrate research and teaching is that it should be reflected in the policies and strategies of its constituent faculties, schools, and departments. Yet policies and strategies merely provide the starting point for development. They are not ends in themselves. Our experience at the University of Sydney was that the extent to which schools and departments encouraged aligning research and teaching varied across the university. Some faculties were encouraging teacher-focused approaches to research-led teaching (such as talking about research in lectures); there were faculties encouraging student-focused approaches (such as the use of inquiry-based projects); and there were faculties attempting to integrate teaching and research not only in specific courses but in departmental organization and the design of whole curricula (such as with problem-based learning). Once again, the value of the working group was in sharing practice across diverse contexts.

A faculty seriously committed to the integration of research and teaching cannot simply rest at the level of a few leading people changing their practice nor at attempts to proselytize new approaches to others. A key challenge for faculties and departments is how to move practice forward. Colbeck (1998) argues that there are a number of contextual factors that influence the extent to which faculty are able to integrate their research and their teaching at an individual level. So, for example, the ways in which research is defined will have an impact. A broad definition of research that includes the Boyer (1990) scholarships of integration, engagement, and teaching will be more easily integrated into teaching than narrowly defined discovery research. Colbeck (1998, 2002) further suggests that in areas where there is a high degree of agreement about research approaches and methods and high levels of research collaboration, such as in the sciences, there is likely to be less opportunity to integrate research than in areas where faculty have a high degree of autonomy and work in an individualistic way, such as in the humanities. Further, the more bureaucratic the institution is, the less faculty are likely to have opportunities to integrate their research and their teaching. The extent to which an academic is able to participate in decisions regarding what they should teach will also have an impact. For example, where faculty are able to choose what they teach they are more likely to choose areas that are in their research interests.

## University Commitment

Evidence of a university's commitment to research and teaching integration comes from an examination of university policies and organization, such as whether teaching and learning policies and research policies include references to the importance of linking research and teaching, and whether there are separate committees for teaching and for research matter. An important issue is how at the institutional level research bodies can be encouraged to see bringing together research and teaching as benefiting both research and teaching. Strong high-level leadership is important. However, if initiatives to bring research and teaching together are driven by the senior person responsible for teaching and learning, not by the senior person responsible for research, the integration of research and teaching is going to be different than at other institutions where there is a deliberate attempt by the senior people responsible for teaching and for research to jointly own a similar initiative.

## Conclusion

Through the initiatives discussed in this chapter, we believe we have made substantial progress in developing understanding of the nature of research-led teaching and what is required to develop it. Progress has been made toward moving people's thinking away from a teacher-focused view of research-led teaching to focus more on the student experience. It remains to be seen how, when, and whether students' learning experiences are enhanced in consequence. University rhetoric is that the university's research record is important in attracting the best students. However, more still needs to be known about how students view research in the university, what experiences of research they have, how their learning experiences and outcomes can be enhanced, and what effect their views have on the quality of their experiences of research.

The University of Sydney statement of what is meant by research-led teaching and the scholarship of teaching emphasizes the idea of a partnership between students and faculty. I believe such a partnership is the cornerstone to bringing research and teaching together. There is still much to learn about what doing that can offer students and how it can enhance academic work, but it is already evident from our experience at the University of Sydney that the marriage of institutional policy and strategy together with informed pedagogical input, at the very least, can develop understanding of how to bring research and teaching closer together. To move a whole university in that direction takes a lot of time and effort. But if higher education is likely as a consequence to prepare students more effectively for professional life in the twenty-first century, the effort will have been worth it.

New Directions for Teaching and Learning • DOI: 10.1002/tl

## References

Boyer, E. L. *Scholarship Revisited.* Stanford, Calif.: Carnegie Foundation for the Advancement of Teaching, 1990.

Brew, A. "Teaching and Research: New Relationships and Their Implications for Inquiry-Based Teaching and Learning in Higher Education." *Higher Education Research and Development,* 2003, 22(1), 3–18.

Brew, A. *Research and Teaching: Beyond the Divide.* London: Palgrave Macmillan, 2006.

Colbeck, C. "Merging in a Seamless Blend: How Faculty Integrate Teaching and Research." *Journal of Higher Education,* 1998, 69(6), 647–671.

Colbeck, C. "Balancing Teaching with Other Responsibilities: Integrating Roles or Feeding Alligators." Paper presented at the Annual Meeting of the American Educational Research Association, Penn State University, 2002.

Dwyer, C. "Linking Research and Teaching: A Staff-Student Interview Project." *Journal of Geography in Higher Education,* 2001, 25(3), 357–366.

Gibbons, M., and others. *The New Production of Knowledge: The Dynamics of Science and Research in Contemporary Societies.* Thousand oaks, Calif.: Sage, 1994.

Hattie, J. "Performance Indicators for the Interdependence of Research and Teaching." In P. Shelley and G. Suddaby (eds.), *Towards Understanding the Interdependence of Research and Teaching: Occasional Papers from the Vice-Chancellor's Symposium on the Research Teaching Nexus.* Palmerston North, New Zealand: Massey University, 2001.

Jenkins, A., Blackman, T., Lindsay, R., and Paton-Saltzberg, R. "Teaching and Research: Student Perspectives and Policy Implications." *Studies in Higher Education,* 1998, 23(2), 127–141.

Jenkins, A., and Zetter, R. *Linking Research and Teaching in Departments.* Oxford: LTSN Generic Centre, Learning and Teaching Support Network, Oxford Brookes University, 2003.

Prosser, M., and Trigwell, K. *Understanding Learning and Teaching: The Experience in Higher Education.* Maidenhead, United Kingdom: Society for Research into Higher Education and Open University Press, 1999.

University of Sydney. *Strategic Directions, 2005–2010.* Sydney, Australia: University of Sydney, 2005. http://www.usyd.edu.au/about/publication/strategic/2006/index.shtml. Accessed Aug. 3, 2006.

Zamorski, B. "Research-Led Teaching and Learning in Higher Education: A Case." *Teaching in Higher Education,* 2002, 7(4), 411–427.

Zetter, R. "Getting from Perkins to Jenkins: Filling the Implementation Gap." *Teaching News, The Newsletter of Oxford Brookes University,* Feb. 5–6, 2002.

ANGELA BREW *is associate professor at the Institute for Teaching and Learning at the University of Sydney, Australia.*

NEW DIRECTIONS FOR TEACHING AND LEARNING • DOI: 10.1002/tl

# 3

*An Academic Practice Unit needs to work strategically and interact with other departments to place research-based teaching on the institutional agenda and support staff adequately for their roles.*

# Professional Development Support to Promote Stronger Teaching and Research Links

*Andrew J. Castley*

Five perspectives on research-based teaching are commonly distinguished. Respectively, they focus on *outcome,* whereby staff introduce their undergraduate students to their own research via a simple transmission process; *tools,* whereby students typically take a "research methods" module as part of their course; *process,* whereby students undertake a significant amount of learning through inquiry; *context,* whereby the department as a whole develops an ethos in which students feel themselves to be a part of a community of learners, including through research; and *pedagogy,* whereby learning and teaching in the discipline or the department becomes the subject of research (Baxter Magolda, 1999; Brew, 2003).

Part Two of this volume is concerned largely with developing or researching the "process" dimension of research-based teaching, while Part Three is concerned with the pedagogy aspect. Part One takes an overall view, and this chapter will deal specifically with the way an academic practice unit (APU) can support academics to develop research-based teaching in the various ways these relationships may be conceptualized. In contrast to centers of teaching and learning (that come under many different names), an academic practice unit, as the term itself suggests, supports academics not only in their teaching role but also, ideally, in their various roles associated with the broader notion of academic practice.

NEW DIRECTIONS FOR TEACHING AND LEARNING, no. 107, Fall 2006   © Wiley Periodicals, Inc.
Published online in Wiley InterScience (www.interscience.wiley.com) • DOI: 10.1002/tl.241

In many institutions, the outcome, tools, process, context, and peda-gogical perspectives can be found in existing arrangements. Efforts that can be observed include matching staff's research interests with their teaching, offering a research methods component in courses and programs, or involv-ing students in inquiry-based learning through midcourse projects and final-year dissertations. The ethos of research-led departments will tend to rub off on students. In very recent times, increasing resources are being devoted to researching and developing learning and teaching in all disciplines. Strengthening the research-teaching link may, to an extent, be no more than making explicit these existing practices, using the vocabulary of research-based teaching.

This chapter considers a variety of approaches to strengthening the overt links between research and teaching by combining systems and human interaction strategies.

## Some Challenges

There are a number of forces that mitigate the influence an academic prac-tice unit (APU) that seeks to strengthen the links between teaching and research might have. First, in research-led institutions, relatively little time is given by core staff to teaching, which often leaves little scope for experi-menting with, for example, inquiry-based learning or conducting research into the merits of transmission versus other curriculum models.

Second, the case for strengthening research and teaching links is not uncontested. Hattie and Marsh (1996), in a study of the research, found no conclusive evidence that research-active staff taught more effectively than staff not active in research.

Third, as Robertson and Bond (2001) reported, in disciplines with a very hierarchical knowledge structure, staff perceived that the relationship between teaching and research could only be activated at the postgraduate level. They felt that at the undergraduate level students "lacked the disciplinary frame-work to engage in enquiry" (p. 11). This position may well not be universally shared; but where it prevails, the APU has to recognize and cope with it.

Fourth, what counts as research affects staff perceiving positive rela-tionships between their involvement in their research and their teaching. It is likely that staff in strong research institutions will value discovery research of the sort rewarded in the Research Assessment Exercise (RAE). (The RAE is the key mechanism for distributing research funding in the United Kingdom, based on peer review.) Less research-oriented institutions may value the scholarships of application and teaching (Boyer, 1990), for example the production of teaching materials like textbooks and software (Colbeck, 1998).

Fifth and finally, the Research Assessment Exercise in the United Kingdom led to a gradual separation of research from teaching. McNay (1999) reported departmental heads as saying that good researchers spend less time teaching, and more undergraduate teaching is done by part-timers and postgraduates.

For all these reasons, any APU wishing to promote stronger research-teaching links on campus needs to identify its positioning, remit, and resourcing, and to devise its strategy carefully.

## Setting the Institutional Agenda

What can an APU do to raise research-based teaching on the institutional agenda? In some institutional contexts it may be appropriate for a senior figure to commit the institution to research-led learning. Whether or not such commitment is forthcoming, the institutional learning, teaching, and research strategies (an institutional strategic plan aimed at organizing, maintaining, and enhancing teaching and research quality) constitute a potentially powerful lever to develop research-based teaching. Such strategies should make explicit reference to research-based teaching and contain, for example, a brief description of the various dimensions of research-based teaching in the terms referred to above. Since the purpose of research-based teaching is to bridge the research-teaching divide, cross-membership of a learning and teaching committee and a research committee is a natural infrastructural arrangement to pursue this agenda. It may also be possible to introduce occasional agenda items on both committees in parallel, or include the agenda as an aspect of a standing item such as staff development.

There are a number of ways in which an APU can act through the incentive mechanisms operated by the university. These might include appraisal, promotion on the basis (partly) of teaching, and internal teaching awards. In each case, the relevant protocol would include research, learning and teaching, and an informed approach to linking the two.

An appropriately positioned APU may act within a quality assurance context to promote research-based teaching as an institutional priority. Course approval and course or departmental review protocols could include staff's views and practices of research-based teaching. APU personnel could work together with academic departments coming up for cyclical or external review over a period of, say, eighteen months, as part of the university's standard quality assurance and enhancement arrangements.

## Helping People Meet the Agenda

This section considers possible actions in three categories of a dissemination strategy: dissemination for awareness, dissemination for understanding, and dissemination for action (Stewart and Thompson, 2005).

**Why Do It?** Like anybody else, academics need reasons for doing things. These motivations will depend on the strategic mission of the institution, the orientation of particular departments, external agendas to which the institution wants to respond, and the position of individuals and groups of academic staff within departments.

*Some Outcomes-Based Reasons for Linking Research and Teaching.* Some assumptions we may reasonably make about the benefits of working with academics to promote teaching-research synergies include the following:

- It raises students' awareness of the research-oriented ways in which they are learning (referred to as meta-learning).
- It makes students feel part of a learning community, in which research and teaching are seen as part and parcel of the same endeavor.
- It increases motivation of students through active, or inquiry-based, learning.
- It increases staff's motivation by achieving synergies between their teaching and learning.
- It increases research output in both disciplinary and pedagogic research by pursuing research-based teaching approaches.
- It improves students' results profile.
- It develops students' autonomy in learning, which translates in other contexts into their being self-starters.
- It sensitizes students to their academic potential beyond their first degree.
- The institution may gain recognition for and benefit from publicizing good, inclusive academic practice.

*A Theoretical Reason.* Current perspectives on knowledge use draw from a theory of learning known as *constructivism,* which sees the learner as an active constructor of his or her own knowledge and meaning rather than as a more passive receiver of information and expertise (Hutchinson and Huberman, 1993). In the "harder" rather than the "softer" disciplines, where academics may not be so ready to accept this proposition, the constructivist case can perhaps be made for the higher cognitive operations. The tools of the trade—axioms, theorems, the characteristics of materials and natural phenomena, and so on—may be most pragmatically learned through transmission approaches. But at higher levels of learning, such as application, integration, and synthesis, the articulation of problems and their elegant or efficient solutions seem to be susceptible to explanation in constructivist terms and learnable through research-like (that is, inquiry-based) activities.

*A Reason from Student Motivation.* There is overwhelming evidence that learning through doing is far more effective than learning through being told. Reasons include that action is a multisensory experience, that in doing learners directly discover the utility of knowledge, and that in seeing that knowledge works the student is relieved of the necessity to take someone else's word for it (Jenkins, Breen, and Lindsay, 2003).

*Are We Doing It Already?* In many departments, there is likely to be already much practice that could be described in terms of research-based teaching. The processes underpinning personal profiling, work-placement learning, skills development, employability programs, project and dissertation work, and so on may be so described. In research-oriented universities, people may think of research in terms of "the scholarship of discovery" (Boyer, 1990). The discussion around what counts as research-based teaching and where the boundaries should be drawn could potentially be very productive and result in an enhancement of some learning and teaching approaches.

The importance of thinking through this question of what is research-based teaching and presenting it powerfully is that academic staff need sound reasons for devoting their energies to change.

## Dissemination for Awareness

Five strategies are suggested that an APU might employ to raise awareness about different dimensions of research-based teaching.

- The APU might establish a steering group comprised mainly of staff from academic departments to develop such an initiative.
- APU staff may undertake a survey of departments to identify current practices that align with research-based teaching. The exercise would initiate a repository of cases for further dissemination.
- APU staff could establish a reference list of sources for later use.
- Web pages could be publicized that carry a brief conceptual overview of the aspects of research-based teaching (for example, that of Warwick University at http://www2.warwick.ac.uk/services/cap/eddev/rbl/whatis) and relate research-based teaching to the institutional context, provide links to further references, and offer brief case studies.
- Internal educational development publications can provide fuller expositions of research-based teaching and its rationale.

## Dissemination for Understanding

In this second phase, academic staff deepen their engagement with the various possibilities in pursuit of the aims outlined above. Measures to achieve this deepening might include the following:

- APU staff attend departmental meetings to publicize the initiative. In this way, the APU will be able to gauge reception of its initiative among staff and adjust its approach and materials accordingly.
- The APU could mount an annual learning and teaching conference, which could contain a strand or keynote address on research-based teaching.
- Institution-wide professional development programs for staff could include a section on research-based teaching.

NEW DIRECTIONS FOR TEACHING AND LEARNING • DOI: 10.1002/tl

- To take the initiative further, a network of interested academics from different departments could be built. The network might be supported by meetings, a weblog, or Web forum.
- Published case studies of students' first-hand accounts with inquiry-based learning can serve as powerful illustrators and persuaders, and effort could usefully be given to building a repository of research-based teaching cases.
- Case studies of academic staff's pedagogical research projects (often completed as part of a professional development program) could be motivating (see also Chapter Eight in this volume).

A publicized, intensive project to produce a repository of research-based teaching cases is likely not only to achieve its main aim but also to raise awareness of research-based teaching perspectives among staff generally.

If the APU can win external funding to develop a detailed resource, so much the better. Winning such awards is part and parcel of what successful disciplinary academics do. This will help to secure the credentials of the APU and its initiative. One example of such an initiative is the TELRI project at Warwick University. The Web site of this project includes detailed guidelines on reviewing and developing a course to incorporate research-based teaching (http://www.warwick.ac.uk/ETS/TELRI).

In all of these activities, as Stewart and Thompson (2005) say, the initiative should not be seen as "educational-development led," but be owned by the academic community. A steering group comprising mainly teaching academics, which meets occasionally, might serve this aim well.


## Dissemination for Action

This phase focuses on the work of APU staff and academics at close quarters and is meant to lead to changes in curriculum.

**Working at Close Quarters.** Working "at close quarters" means, among other things, providing ongoing, interactive, personal contact with intended users. Professional and personal relationships of respect and trust between people in academic departments and people in the APU are essential. The following perspectives are adapted from the National Center for the Dissemination of Disability Research (1996).

People tend to trust sources with whom they have established relationships. For example, if the academic department has a teaching fellow interested in research-based teaching—especially if the person is seconded to the APU for some time—this person would be key to engaging others within the department. Alternatively, the APU may broker the services of an external subject specialist able to offer experience of research-based teaching in the discipline concerned.

Change in professional practice, which is embodied in a shift to inquiry-based learning, is in itself a process of learning. Readiness to change is a state of mind that involves, first, people's perception that change is needed, and second, their willingness to overcome fears, doubts, and other resistances in order to make that change.

It is important to be aware of the forms of scholarship staff espouse and value (discovery, application, synthesis, teaching, according to Boyer, 1990), and which curriculum models they are used to (transmission, constructivism, personal development). Indeed, much will depend on the level of awareness or tolerance staff have for these educational concepts.

Academic staff will want to be at least codrivers of any development. Collaborative, or action research, in which APU staff and departmental academics jointly plan and conduct pedagogical research activities, may be a way of approaching change. In a larger department, an advisory committee may be useful as a way of centering ownership of the development squarely among academic staff.

Another common way in which APU staff might engage academic colleagues may be as a valued fly on the wall, offering examples of approaches from elsewhere. If advice is offered, it should be done with great circumspection.

**Maximizing the Return from Funded Initiatives.** Under "setting the institutional agenda," we referred to the possibility of writing research-based teaching into funded initiatives, such as teaching awards and projects organized within a funded learning and teaching strategy. In addition, departments themselves are likely to attract external funding in connection with teaching learning and assessment. With reference to the pedagogical dimension of research-based teaching, in all these cases the APU could approach the staff involved to explore the possibility of (co-) authoring a paper looking at the relevant pedagogy. The APU will be well placed to contribute the wider context, while the disciplinary academic is likely to be able and willing to focus on the immediate impact of the development in question. In this way, an ethos of research-informed, evidence-based pedagogy can be fostered over time.

## Working with Graduate Teaching Assistants

Particularly in research-led institutions, first- and second-year undergraduates are increasingly taught by graduate teaching assistants (GTAs). As the student's role as critical purchaser of educational services becomes more pronounced in an increasingly marketized higher education sector, the arrangements for supporting GTAs, often from overseas and still having to establish themselves in their demanding facilitative role, will come increasingly under scrutiny (Castley, 2005).

Where the academic practice unit provides training and development for GTAs, either collaboratively with academic departments or centrally, this channel can be used to encourage GTAs to share their own research with their undergraduate students. In the often more interactive mode in which GTA teaching takes place, undergraduate students may be able to gain insight into and enthusiasm for what it's like to do research from a person who is likely to be much closer to them in terms of age as well as life and professional experience.

Several research-led universities in the United Kingdom have followed the Stanford (U.S.) practice of funding undergraduate research projects. Warwick's Undergraduate Research Scholarship Scheme (URSS—http://www2.warwick.ac.uk/services/cap/curriculum/RBL/URSS) is operated by the university's APU, designated the Center for Academic Practice (CAP). The scheme invites applications from staff for a stipend to support a piece of research. The stipend holders will normally be second-year students who typically pursue a ten-week research project under supervision, often in the summer. Stipends range from £700 (US$1,300) to £1,600 (US$3,000). The high-quality poster exhibition of the work done, mounted annually in October, is highly valued by participating departments and nonparticipants alike.

The application, adjudication, recording, and reporting processes are rigorous. The students are supported individually by their disciplinary supervisor and collectively by CAP staff. The stipend holders meet twice informally prior to undertaking their projects, once for a review session, and finally at the October exhibition. Participants avail themselves of the dedicated weblog. All these activities are aimed at creating a community of inquiry centered on the scheme.

Projects frequently culminate in a joint paper, review, or conference presentation with the student's supervisor. Participating students are invariably enthused by the experience, many being significantly influenced in their proposed career direction.

Similar schemes are run at Cambridge University and Imperial College London. Both are referred to as UROP (Undergraduate Research Opportunities Program—http://www.imperial.ac.uk/urop/). At Warwick the work of the URSS is, at the time of writing, being significantly augmented with the advent of the Center for Excellence in Teaching and Learning, called the Reinvention Center for Undergraduate Research (http://www2.warwick.ac.uk/fac/soc/sociology/research/cetl/). The Reinvention Center includes in its program the funding of inquiry-based learning projects within academic departments.

## Concluding Comments

This chapter covered a range of approaches and interventions to support research-based teaching. The key factors for success seem to be the credibility of the staff of the APU and others associated with the initiative, departmental ownership of any research-based teaching projects, the diversity in the interpretation and implementation of research-based teaching, and the integration of research-based teaching initiatives into the institutional strategic plan.

Research-based teaching is probably widely practiced already in different ways. It may be considered of value to make this fact explicit for student motivation and for the outward-facing purposes of publicity and audit.

# References

Baxter Magolda, M. B. *Impact of the Undergraduate Summer School Experience on Epistemological Development.* Oxford, Ohio: University of Miami, 1999.

Boyer, E. L. *Scholarship Revisited.* Stanford, Calif.: Carnegie Foundation for the Advancement of Teaching, 1990.

Brew, A. "Teaching and Research: New Relationships and Their Implications for Inquiry-Based Teaching and Learning in Higher Education." *Higher Education Research and Development,* 2003, 22(1), 3–18.

Castley, A. "Graduate Teaching Assistants." *Educational Developments,* 2005, 6(3).

Colbeck, C. L. "Merging in a Seamless Blend: How Faculty Integrate Teaching and Research." *Journal of Higher Education,* 1998, 69(6), 647–671.

Hattie, J., and Marsh, H. W. "The Relationship Between Research and Teaching: A Meta-Analysis." *Review of Educational Research,* 1996, 66(4), 507–542.

Hutchinson, J., and Huberman, M. *Knowledge Dissemination and Utilization in Science and Mathematics Education: A Literature Review.* Washington, D.C.: National Science Foundation, 1993.

Jenkins, A., Breen, R., and Lindsay, R., with Brew, A. *Re-Shaping Higher Education: Linking Teaching and Research.* London: Kogan Page, 2003.

McNay, I. "The Paradoxes of Research Assessment and Funding." In M. Henkel and B. Little (eds.), *Changing Relations Between Higher Education and the State.* London: Jessica Kingsley, 1999.

National Center for the Dissemination of Disability Research. *Improving Links Between Research and Practice: Improving the Usefulness of Disability Research: A Toolbox of Dissemination Strategies. Guides to Improving Practice 2.* Austin, Tex.: National Center for the Dissemination of Disability Research, 1996. http://www.ncddr.org/du/products/guide2.html. Accessed Sept. 2005.

Robertson, J., and Bond, C. "Experiences of the Relation Between Teaching and Research: What Do Academics Value?" *Higher Education Research and Development,* 2001, 20(1), 5–19.

Stewart, M., and Thompson, S. "Developing a Dissemination Strategy." *Educational Developments,* 2005, 6(2).

*ANDREW J. CASTLEY is an academic development adviser at Warwick University, where he leads the university's Undergraduate Research Scholarship Scheme.*

NEW DIRECTIONS FOR TEACHING AND LEARNING • DOI: 10.1002/tl

# PART TWO

Research-Based Teaching as Student-Focused, Inquiry-Based Learning

4

*We now have pedagogical methods that can be successful—
that is, effective—with most students at the undergraduate
stage; one very promising method is problem-based or
inquiry-based learning.*

# The Nature of Effective or Exemplary Teaching in an Environment That Emphasizes Strong Research and Teaching Links

*Lewis Elton*

The words *effective* and *exemplary* in the title of this chapter are important. The first implies that such teaching leads to effective learning; the
second implies that it can serve as a model for practicing teachers. Ideally, neither commits the common failing that there is such a thing as best teaching,
irrespective of circumstances, or that practicing teachers should simply adopt
a proposed model. Teaching—and learning—are idiosyncratic activities, in
which to adapt rather than to adopt should be the guide for both teachers and
learners. The constraint, that teaching—and presumably learning—takes
place in an environment that emphasizes strong research and teaching links,
is equally important. That all teaching should be based on underlying and relevant research should not need emphasizing, but that the teaching environment itself should emphasize strong research and teaching links raises the
question as to whether such links are essential for effective teaching. In
general, the answer to that question must surely be in the negative, but the
argument of the present chapter—and it is contentious—will be that it is
essential for teaching at university level, with which we are concerned.

Before the advent of mass higher education, universities were faced,
broadly speaking, with two kinds of students: the scholarship boys and those
for whom the university was a finishing school. (There were few girls in those

NEW DIRECTIONS FOR TEACHING AND LEARNING, no. 107, Fall 2006   © Wiley Periodicals, Inc.
Published online in Wiley InterScience (www.interscience.wiley.com) • DOI: 10.1002/tl.242

distant days, but they were likely to be in the scholarship group.) The nomenclature is that of Oxford and Cambridge, where highly competitive entrance examinations—for rich and poor alike—were used for prestige reasons for all, as well as to provide financial support for the poor. These were the students on whom their teachers—largely through the famous Oxbridge tutorial system (Ashwin, 2005)—concentrated their effort, seeing in them their successors, while the rest of the student body—the finishing-school type—tended to be coached through their examinations. Other countries—those that relied essentially on the mass lecture as the main teaching medium—had less sharp divisions between the two groups and mostly had less financial support for the scholarly one or personal support for either. A good example of the teaching in this latter mode in the nineteenth century comes from the recorded experience of the students of Mendeléyev in Russia: "His lecture room was always thronged with students. 'Many of them,' writes one of these, 'I am afraid could not follow Mendeléyev, but for the few of us who could it was a stimulant to the intellect and a lesson in scientific thinking which must have left deep traces in their development'" (Encyclopaedia Britannica, 1929, *15*, 241).

In the more developed system in Germany, where the seminar had been introduced as early as the eighteenth century, it is apparent (Paulsen, 1908) that its main purpose was "to introduce the student into scientific[1] research," that is, it was designed—just as in the case of Mendeléyev—for future researchers and by implication, for future academics.

The advent of mass higher education, where universities have an equal responsibility to all their students, has made such elitist approaches no longer appropriate, but unless very active steps are taken to introduce change, there is a considerable danger that the methods formerly applied essentially only to the intellectual elite will be applied to all. When this approach will inevitably fail, there is an even greater danger that these methods will be abandoned and replaced by dumbed down methods that will postpone real learning into the postgraduate period; that is, it will again be reserved for a selected minority. It is the purpose of this chapter to suggest that we now have methods that can be successful—that is, effective—with most students at the undergraduate stage.

## Forms of Effective or Exemplary Teaching

On the basis of the widely accepted assumption that there should be a research-teaching nexus for effective or exemplary teaching at the university level, this nexus can be expressed in several ways:

1. The charismatic lecture by a leading researcher
2. The vicarious experience of a student being taught traditionally by a researcher
3. Teaching associated with research by undergraduates
4. Teaching that leads to learning in a research mode

These teaching approaches will be treated in turn and discussed more fully below; the topic of the nexus between research and teaching is discussed more generally in Elton (2001).

The first approach is the most common form. Its pros and cons come out clearly from the work of practitioners such as Faraday and Bragg (1974). Its effect is mainly motivational and often limited to the best students, where best is defined as those who in due course become professors (Elton, 2001).

The second approach, as discussed by Hodgson (1997), is really a variant of the first—less dramatic, but possibly more effective. It relates to traditional teaching carried out by teachers who are researchers in the field and thus are able to relate their teaching explicitly to their own research.

The third approach is very common and indeed can be very successful in the final year of a course in the form of project work, but it is dangerous to base whole courses on it, even for the best students. Thus, the attempt at MIT to introduce undergraduate research (in the Undergraduate Research Opportunities Program) at the very beginning of undergraduate courses proved a failure—even the highly motivated and able MIT students apparently were not able to cope with it.

The fourth approach is the only form that can successfully form the basis of a whole curriculum. While it was inherent in Humboldt's prescription for teaching in universities,[2] it was not fully realized (for all disciplines and all years) until the advent of problem-based learning and its relation, inquiry-based learning. Discussion of it will constitute the most significant part of this chapter.

The chapter will end with a discussion of how effective or exemplary teaching can be recognized; it will be argued that such recognition requires a professionalism that is rare in a profession that does not consider formal professional development necessary or even appropriate.

## The Limitations of the First Three Approaches

The first approach is based on the belief that lecturing can in general be effective beyond the transmission of knowledge. Bragg based his advice on his experience with the famous Royal Institution lectures, the aims of which were inspirational and not the transfer of knowledge (Faraday and Bragg, 1974). Undoubtedly, they could be effective in this way, but Bragg's implication that the model was equally valid for normal lecturing is contradicted by experience, as was recognized by Feynman (1963), one of the great practitioners of the inspirational lecture. For that reason, Hodgson's variant (the second approach) of vicarious experiences that provided stimuli within the format of the traditional university lecture may well be more effective, or at least effective for more students. However, Feynman's reference to Gibbon (1737–1794) that "the power of instruction is seldom of much efficacy, except in those happy dispositions where it is almost superfluous" should always be kept in mind; teaching the most able is the easy part of teaching; it does not absolve teachers from the harder task of teaching all.

In contrast, the success of the third approach, project work that at times is close to research, is beyond doubt when carried out in the final year of a course, but the argument that students can only do such work once they have been through a traditional course and learned their "stuff" is patently false, since good project work is carried out in primary schools. However, what university teachers, for example those at MIT, failed to appreciate and what is blindingly obvious once it is accepted that project work can be carried out also in primary schools, is the pedagogical point that the level of work must be adjusted to the developmental level of the student; that is, it must be at the appropriate level of sophistication. Perhaps there is, after all, some pedagogy that university teachers ought to know about.

## The Fourth Approach and the Shift from Teaching to Learning

A letter writer to the *Times Higher* (1995) stated, "I am not a teacher. I am not employed as a teacher, and I do not wish to be a teacher. I am employed as a lecturer, and in my naivety I thought that my job was to 'know' my field, contribute to it by research, and to lecture on my specialism. Students may attend my lectures but the onus to learn is on them. It is my job to teach them."

How common this attitude is of separating learning and learners from teaching and teachers is not known, but it is useful to understand this point of view if one wants to change it (even if the example reported starts with a claim that a lecturer is not a teacher and ends with the statement that his "job is to teach them"). And change it we want to, to Humboldt's view that "the teacher is not there for the sake of the student, both have their justification in the service of scholarship," and beyond it to a view of cooperation between teacher and student in the service of learning (Elton, 2001, p. 44). In this view—and it is the view that I want to present—the teacher becomes (in the not wholly felicitous phrase) a "facilitator of learning." This dethroning of teachers from their position of being *in* authority—without of course ever losing their role of being *an* authority—is one that many teachers find very difficult, but it is an essential part of the change process that they must undergo. It is paralleled by the need for students to undergo a similar change—from the acceptance of the view that authority with regard to knowledge rests with teachers (Perry, 1970) to the view that learning is a cooperative endeavor between teachers and students. Students arrive—quite justifiably—at university with the former view and it is during the first few weeks at university that it is easiest to convert them to the latter view and abuse them of the idea that university is just like school, only faster; once they believe in that idea—and the practice of lecturing does much to reinforce this view—it is very difficult to change. The issue has been discussed extensively for the important case of English Literature in *Arts and Humanities in Higher Education*, Volumes 2 to 4, particularly Marland (2003). It was this part of the necessary shift that Humboldt failed to appreciate, although it is as old as Lao Tse, who is reputed to have said that "of the best teachers his students say: 'We did it all ourselves.'"

## Problem-Based Learning and Inquiry-Based Learning

Although there are several known approaches to a student-centered curriculum, the one that has proved most effective is problem-based learning (PBL). The literature is huge, but a good start can be made on the basis of Savin-Baden's publications (Savin-Baden and Major, 2004) and earlier works by Savin-Baden quoted there, and its derivative of inquiry-based learning (EBL) (Hutchings and O'Rourke, 2002). The former started forty years ago in a far from pedagogic way—the McMaster University Medical School in Canada was looking for a curriculum that produced medical graduates with more effective diagnostic skills—but by now PBL has been successful in a very large number of disciplines. In the process, the fundamental qualities of PBL have been clarified, as follows:

- A PBL program covers a particular set of learning outcomes (like any other curriculum)
- This outcome is achieved through a carefully crafted set of real problems within the sophistication level of the learners, the solution of which lead to this set of learning outcomes
- Disciplinary knowledge therefore arises from solutions of sets of problems and not from an accumulation of basic knowledge
- The problems are mostly tackled in groups
- Assessment must be in part positivist and in part constructivist, with the latter given a weight corresponding to its importance and not to its reliability. Positivist assessment is appropriate when learning outcomes can be prespecified; constructivist, when this is not possible (Johnston, 2002).

The extension from PBL to EBL arises from the fact that certain disciplines do not have real problems arising from practice; an important extension was to English literature (Hutchings and O'Rourke, 2002). In such disciplines problems are constructed by students, in contrast with the traditional approach in which such problems are constructed by teachers and simply presented to students to solve, with corresponding loss of a sense of ownership on the part of the students. Both those disciplines that have real problems and those that do not share the feature that nothing happens unless the learners initiate it, but in both the role of the learning facilitators is crucial.[3] The student-centeredness is very real and yet the learning could not proceed without a careful input from teachers; just as the saying of Lao

NEW DIRECTIONS FOR TEACHING AND LEARNING • DOI: 10.1002/tl

Tse quoted earlier was the students' view, that of their teacher may well have been different.

All four of the modes discussed provide links between teaching and research and to that extent all—within their respective limitations—are valuable, but only the last does so for all students and at all times. It is the best answer we know at present to Humboldt's demand for *forschendes Lernen* (research-like learning). Incidentally, the other side of this coin is that any form of school-like learning is inappropriate in universities.

## Research and Teaching

We now turn to the second link in the teaching-learning process referred to at the beginning of the chapter: that all teaching should be based on underlying and relevant research. Where this requirement relates to the teaching-learning process, it cannot be overemphasized that the demand for simplistic and often quantitative verifications of "what works" is totally counterproductive. Such a demand is adapted from a situation in that part of medicine (evidence-based medicine) in which it is possible to isolate single variables and in general test their effectiveness, often against placebos. There are effectively no such situations in education. What is needed primarily is a philosophical approach—conceptual clarification and argumentation (G. Mac-Donald Ross, personal communication, 2005), which combines findings, insights, and speculation, together with reflection on practice (Cowan, 1998). Furthermore, the underlying philosophical stance, that is, the student-centeredness, can only be argued in terms of the relation between the educational process and the values of society; different societal values could easily make teacher-centeredness the appropriate starting point. It could be argued that the present tendency of the British Government toward educational authoritarianism may well be served best by traditional lectures together with firmly structured handouts and prespecified learning outcomes; if so, progressive teachers may have to emigrate, although where to is not clear.

## The Professionalism of Teachers and the Need for Change

We finally turn to the question of whether academics should have a professionalism as teachers in the way that they are professional as researchers; that is, that they have received appropriate professional development or *formation*.[4] University teaching may well now be the only profession that is based entirely on tradition transmitted from generation to generation. Hence, while many academics are extremely conscientious in their teaching role, they are also extremely traditional (I teach as I was taught by people who taught as they had been taught), which, in a climate of rapid societal change is, in the longer term, a prescription for failure. Unfortunately, even those who claim to believe in the scholarship of teaching and learning do not always recognize this contradiction, as is evidenced by present efforts in Britain and the United States when professional development is confined effectively to only the initial training of research students and new academics. Such training—and it can rarely, if at all, rise above the level of training—inevitably and rightly concentrates on making those affected competent in the tasks assigned to them, but although such an approach is appropriate for this purpose, it is an essentially conservative measure—that is, it perpetuates present practice, although ideally at a level of greater competence. However, it is here that the difference between doing things better and doing better things becomes crucial.

## Conclusion

To do things better is a means of strengthening current practice, which is important in the short run. In the longer run, it is counterproductive—it reinforces traditional practices that in the changing climate of higher education become increasingly out of date. This situation leads to the conclusion that practice must change, but it says nothing about what it should change to. To some extent, this is bound to be a step into the unknown, but there is now a sufficient amount known from the scholarship of teaching and learning to provide guidance of what kind of change may be required. Undoubtedly, the most important change that the latter has come to advocate is to shift the primacy in the teaching-learning process from teaching to learning and the central role of the participants in the process from teacher to student. This change not only conflicts radically with the aim of acculturating new academics into the existing system, it also leads to a fundamental change in the philosophy of teaching and learning. It can only be justified on the sound principle that new academics have to fit into the existing system as long as it exists, while at the same time experienced academics—or at least a portion of them—must change it. Inevitably, this change has to take place while the old system is still in operation—we cannot close down universities for a year in order to effect the change.

Thus, real improvements in teaching and learning cannot be based on improvements of present practices; what is required are changed practices (Elton, 1999) based on a sophisticated change strategy and carried out by experienced academics who are open to and keen on change. The resulting changed practices must be based on a much deeper understanding of higher education pedagogy and higher education research than can be acquired through experience. These change agents—and there is much evidence that they constitute a small but significant group in any university (estimates range from 10 to 20 percent)—will require a much more sophisticated process of formation than those in initial training, at the level of or close to that of a master's degree, perhaps based on the principles of action research (see Stefani and Elton, 2002). Such academics are at present discouraged by excessive concentrations at the institutional level on disciplinary research.

Appropriate encouragement, including institutional recognition of and rewards for excellence in the scholarship of teaching and learning, would imbue this group with an attitude toward change appropriate to storming the citadel of traditionalism. Is this expectation realistic or just a pipe dream? Only putting it into practice can tell.

## Notes

1. "Scientific" here is a translation of *wissenschaftlich* and so covers all forms of learning and not only the natural sciences.

2. In his Program for the University of Berlin in 1810 (quoted in Elton, 2001, p. 44), Humboldt wrote: "It is furthermore a peculiarity of the institutions of higher learning that they treat higher learning always in terms of not yet completely solved problems, remaining at all times in a research mode [that is, being engaged in an unceasing process of inquiry]. Schools, in contrast, treat only closed and settled bodies of knowledge. The relationship between teacher and learner is therefore completely different in higher learning from what it is in schools. At the higher level, the teacher is not there for the sake of the student, both have their justification in the service of scholarship."

3. Facilitators react to students in a learning situation and often guide it; they do not take a lead.

4. The French *formation* or the German *Ausbildung* express this required synthesis of training and education in a way that English—with its antithesis of education and training—cannot.

## References

Ashwin, P. "Variation in Students' Experiences of the 'Oxford Tutorial.'" *Higher Education,* 2005, *50*(4), 631–644.

Cowan, J. *On Becoming an Innovative University Teacher.* Maidenhead, United Kingdom: Society for Research into Higher Education and Open University Press, 1998.

Elton, L. "New Ways of Learning in Higher Education: Managing the Change." *Tertiary Education and Management,* 1999, *5,* 207–225.

Elton, L. "Research and Teaching: Conditions for a Positive Link." *Teaching in Higher Education,* 2001, *6,* 43–56.

Encyclopaedia Britannica. "Mendeléyev, D. I." In J. L. Garvin and F. Hooper (eds.), *Encyclopaedia Britannica.* (14th ed.) London: Encyclopaedia Britannica, 1929.

Faraday, M., and Bragg, L. *Advice to Lecturers.* London: Royal Institution of Great Britain, 1974.

Feynman, R. P. *Feynman Lectures on Physics.* Reading, Mass.: Addison-Wesley, 1963.

Gibbon, E. *The History of the Decline and Fall of the Roman Empire.* Allen Lane: Penguin Press, 1994. (Originally published 1776.)

Hodgson, V. "Learning from Lectures." In F. Marton and others (eds.), *The Experience of Learning.* (2nd ed.) Edinburgh: Scottish Academic Press, 1997.

Hutchings, B., and O'Rourke, K. "Problem-Based Learning in Literary Studies." *Arts and Humanities in Higher Education,* 2002, *1,* 73–83.

Johnston, B. "Summative Assessment of Portfolios: An Examination of Different Approaches to Agreement over Outcomes." *Studies in Higher Education,* 2002, *29,* 395–412.

Marland, M. "The Transition from School to University." *Arts and Humanities in Higher Education,* 2003, *2,* 201–211.

Paulsen, F. *The German Universities and University Study.* London: Longman, Green, 1908.

Perry, W. G. *Forms of Intellectual and Ethical Development in the College Years: A Scheme.* Austin, Tex.: Holt, Rinehart and Winston, 1970.

Savin-Baden, M., and Major, C. H. *Foundations of Problem-Based Learning.* Buckingham: Society for Research into Higher Education and Open University Press, 2004.

Stefani, L., and Elton, L. "Continuing Professional Development of Academic Teachers Through Self-Initiated Learning." *Assessment and Evaluation in Higher Education,* 2002, 27, 117–129.

*LEWIS ELTON is honorary professor of higher education at University College London and a visiting professor at the University of Manchester.*

NEW DIRECTIONS FOR TEACHING AND LEARNING • DOI: 10.1002/tl

# 5

*Faculty need to be supported and encouraged to integrate disciplinary research and scholarship into undergraduate courses and programs in ways that are beneficial to their students' learning.*

# Strengthening the Teaching-Research Linkage in Undergraduate Courses and Programs

*Mick Healey, Alan Jenkins*

> The issue is whether lecturers adopt teaching approaches that are likely to foster student experiences that mirror the lecturers' experiences as researchers.
>
> R. Barnett (2000, p. 163)

The curriculum is the central site where teaching-research linkages have to be realized. Important as are national policies, institutional and departmental structures, and faculty understanding and knowledge, all these should have as their central focus supporting the student experience of research. We focus on the undergraduate curriculum not only because it is the core business of most higher education institutions, but also because the research evidence indicates that the challenges to developing effective teaching-research links are greatest at that level (Jenkins, 2004). However, the principles suggested here are also applicable to postgraduate courses.

Our suggestions for creating such links are based on both research evidence and our extensive experience of working with faculty. In summary, they are as follows:

- Start from valuing how faculty see these issues
- Recognize the particular contexts in which faculty are working

NEW DIRECTIONS FOR TEACHING AND LEARNING, no. 107, Fall 2006 © Wiley Periodicals, Inc.
Published online in Wiley InterScience (www.interscience.wiley.com) • DOI: 10.1002/tl.243

- Suggest a language and curriculum framework to explore and enhance faculty's current courses
- Acknowledge and build on disciplinary variations
- Make extensive use of case studies
- Recognize the roles of course teams, departments, and institutions
- Appreciate that linking teaching and discipline-based research is but one approach to course design, although for us it should be one of the distinguishing features of higher education

We concur with Barnett (2000) that the world and our understanding of it are continually being transformed by research-based knowledge and that our task as educators in higher education is to help students and the wider society to cope with this "supercomplexity." This task requires that all students develop an understanding of how research is continually reshaping, supporting, and at the same time undermining our understandings of the world. Yet studies of the undergraduate student experience show that many have a poor grasp of the research that goes on in departments and feel distant from this aspect of university life (Healey, Jordan, Pell, and Short, n.d.; Jenkins, Blackman, Lindsay, and Paton-Salzberg, 1998; Zamorski, 2002).

## Value Where Faculty "Are At"

In our work as change agents in improving student learning, we are often encouraging faculty to move to practices and even values that may at first be foreign to them. In working to shift course design to strengthen teaching-research links, we recommend starting by recognizing and valuing where faculty are at. For most faculty, their own identity is bound up with their sense of themselves as scholars and researchers and with inducting students into their disciplinary understandings of knowledge (Becher and Trowler, 2001; Healey, Jenkins, and Kneale, 2000; Healey and Jenkins, 2003). However, one also needs to recognize that there will be major differences within and between institutions in the extent to which faculty are themselves involved in discipline-based research or see such research as important to their role as teachers. There will also be variations and even conflicts in course teams and departments on this issue. So we are entering sensitive territory, but we are in a country where faculty feel at home. However, although we are entering into their worlds, we are seeking to bring to it our own disciplinary expertise of the research evidence on teaching-research relations.

## Recognize the Particular Contexts

In seeking to bring teaching and research together, we have to recognize the particular contexts in which faculty work, for these shape and limit the possibilities to achieve this goal. The classic nineteenth century Humboldtian model of the teaching-research nexus was based on the idea of a researcher-teacher who worked with a small group of students learning and researching together. Now faculty work in mass higher education systems, where research is highly concentrated and where the extent to which faculty are supported to be teachers and researchers will vary significantly between research-intensive and less research-intensive institutions and departments. We suggest the way forward is to hold onto Humboldt's view that "Universities should treat learning as not yet wholly solved problems and hence always in research mode" (Humboldt, 1970, quoted by Elton, 2005, p. 110); but we must also focus on how the curriculum and the wider student experience support student intellectual development through and about research as learning. We should also recognize that the form of, and the possibilities for, teaching-research connections will vary among institutions, departments, and disciplines (Jenkins, Breen, and Lindsay, 2003). For example, although research or inquiry-based learning is an effective form of learning for students in both research-intensive and less research-intensive institutions and may be facilitated by both more and less research-active faculty, the character of the activity and the opportunities will vary. These two characteristics are influenced by many factors, including the willingness of faculty to engage in this mode of teaching, the departmental and institutional teaching and learning culture, and the research environment and resources available. Students may also need to be convinced of the benefits for them of this form of learning if they are not already familiar with it.

## Suggest a Language and Curricular Framework

For many faculty and educational developers, their initial understanding of linking teaching and research is limited to faculty designing the curriculum around their research expertise. To move beyond this restricted conception of teaching-research links, we need to offer a language and curricular framework that is inclusive of all faculty in all institutions but that is also clearly focused on the student experience and intellectual development.

We have found the framework developed by Griffiths (2004) effective in supporting faculty to examine both their current courses and how to strengthen the links between discipline-based research and teaching. According to Griffiths, teaching can be research-led, research-oriented, or research-based, as characterized by the following:

- Research-led: Where students learn about research findings, the curriculum content is dominated by faculty research interests, and information transmission is the main teaching mode.
- Research-oriented: Where students learn about research processes, the curriculum emphasizes as much the processes by which knowledge is produced as learning knowledge that has been achieved, and faculty try to engender a research ethos through their teaching.

• Research-based: Where students learn as researchers, the curriculum is largely designed around inquiry-based activities, and the division of roles between teacher and student is minimized.

Healey (2005a) has developed Griffiths' framework into a diagrammatic model, shown in Figure 5.1, that highlights the extent to which courses bring students into research as participants and develop their abilities to carry out research. He introduces an additional category—research-tutored—in which the curriculum is focused around students writing essays and discussing ideas with faculty (tutors). Often the most effective learning experiences involve a combination of all four approaches, but we would argue that the emphasis should be placed on the student-centered approaches in the top half of Figure 5.1 (see also Chapter Four in this volume).

In the United States, which has long operated a mass higher education system, the undergraduate research movement, in which "students do hands-on learning often in the company of a faculty mentor" (Kinkead, 2003, p. 1), is often mainly for those students with high grades and motivation. There are also examples of special research opportunity programs supporting minority students to obtain access to and achieve success in uni-

**Figure 5.1. Curriculum Design and the Research-Teaching Nexus**

STUDENT FOCUSED

STUDENTS AS PARTICIPANTS

|  | **Research-Tutored** | **Research-Based** |  |
|---|---|---|---|
| **EMPHASIS ON RESEARCH CONTENT** | Curriculum emphasizes learning focused on students writing and discussing essays and papers | *Curriculum emphasizes students' undertaking inquiry-based learning* | **EMPHASIS ON RESEARCH PROCESSES AND PROBLEMS** |
|  | **Research-Led** | **Research-Oriented** |  |
|  | *Curriculum is structured around teaching current subject content* | Curriculum emphasizes teaching processes of knowledge construction in the subject |  |

TEACHER FOCUSED

STUDENTS AS AUDIENCE

*Source:* Healey (2005, p. 70).

NEW DIRECTIONS FOR TEACHING AND LEARNING • DOI: 10.1002/tl

versity studies (Jenkins and Healey, 2005). The challenge is how to develop research experiences for all students. A range of strategies faculty may use is given in Exhibit 5.1.

## Acknowledge and Build on Disciplinary Variations

While introducing faculty to the generic research and scholarship on teaching-research relations, it is also important to support them in considering the features of their discipline area that make teaching-research relations distinctive (see also Chapter Seven in this volume). Clearly, this is an area

### Exhibit 5.1. Strategies for Linking Teaching and Research Within Courses and Programs.

Strategy 1: Develop Students' Understanding of the Role of Research in their Discipline(s)
- Develop the curriculum to bring out current or previous research developments in the discipline
- Develop students' awareness of learning from faculty involvement in research
- Develop students' understanding of how research is organized and funded in the discipline, institution, and profession

Strategy 2: Develop Students' Abilities to Carry Out Research
- Students learn in ways that mirror research processes
- Assess students in ways that mirror research processes (for example, by requiring students to have their work assessed by peers according to the house style of a journal before submitting it to you)
- Provide training in relevant research skills and knowledge
- Ensure students experience courses that require them to do research projects, and that there is a progressive move to projects of greater complexity
- Develop student involvement in faculty research

Strategy 3: Progressively Develop Students' Understanding
- Ensure that introductory courses induct students into the role of research in their discipline and present knowledge as created, uncertain, and contested
- Ensure that advanced courses develop students' understanding of research and progressively develop their capacities to do research
- Ensure that graduating-year courses require students to carry out a major research study and help them to integrate their understanding of the role of research in their discipline or interdisciplines

Strategy 4: Manage Student Experience of Faculty Research
- Limit the negative consequences for students of faculty involvement in research. Most important here is managing the student experience of the days (and sabbatical terms) when faculty are "away" doing research.
- Evaluate students' experience of research and feed that back into the curriculum
- Make clear to students the employability elements of research. This action is particularly important for those students whose focus is on using a degree to get employment—and who may not otherwise appreciate the value of a research-based approach.

Based on Jenkins, Breen, and Lindsay (2003, pp. 63–64).

where discipline-based faculty have expertise (Healey, 2005b), which should be valued and extended by presenting frameworks, such as the distinctions Biglan (1973) makes between pure and applied and hard and soft disciplines. For example, this literature indicates that teaching the latest research findings is more challenging in so-called hard disciplines such as mathematics because of the more hierarchical nature of knowledge construction than in soft disciplines such as history (Healey, 2005a). In contrast, it is more common for students to work with faculty on research projects in the laboratory science subjects than in the humanities. Recognition of the role of professional associations in facilitating or impeding the teaching-research nexus is also important, particularly in vocational subjects.

## Examine Case Studies

A key way to enhance teaching-research links is for faculty to analyze case studies from both their own discipline and other disciplines, for these give them a lens through which to analyze their own practices and consider how they could be developed. Exhibit 5.2 presents summaries of a few of the case studies that we use when working with faculty. Some of these cases studies come from a project run with a selection of the twenty-four United Kingdom Subject Centers (national, discipline-based teaching and learning centers), which aimed to identify discipline-based practices for linking teaching and research (http://www.heacademy.ac.uk/850.htm). This work is currently being extended, as part of a United Kingdom Higher Education Academy project, to most of the remaining Centers.

### Exhibit 5.2. Discipline Case Studies.

Biology Research Experiences

*At Cornell University, in the United States, all first-year biologists have research experiences.* The Explorations Program introduces biology first-year undergraduates to research by Cornell faculty in the context of a course of seven hundred to nine hundred students. Large-scale funding has created between 100 and 120 "experiences," each of approximately three to four hours, for groups of six to eight students. Most are designed to introduce students to the kinds of research problems on which faculty work. Programs take place both in research labs on campus and at field sites near campus. The program is structured so that each student is required to participate in one exploration per semester.
http://ws.cc.stonybrook.edu/Reinventioncenter/spotlight.html; http://biog-101-104.bio.cornell.edu/BioG101_104/explorations/explorations.html

*Publishing undergraduate research in an extracurricular house journal*
At the University of Chester, United Kingdom, the Department of Biological Sciences operates an undergraduate journal, called *Origin*, to publish research work completed by students. In contrast to the many U.S. institutions with undergraduate research programs, here the focus is at course team or department level.
http://www.bioscience.heacademy.ac.uk/projects/tdf/potter.htm

NEW DIRECTIONS FOR TEACHING AND LEARNING • DOI: 10.1002/tl

*Asking Questions in Plant Biology at Australian National University*
A practical exercise designed for a Level 2 course involves students making observations in a botanical garden; coming up with ten questions each (such as, why do eucalyptus leaves dangle?), and coming up as a group with hypotheses based on the questions; thinking of ways of testing the hypotheses; and writing up individually their ten questions and one hypothesis as a 750-word mini-proposal for a research project.
http://www.anu.edu.au/CEDAM/ilearn/inquiry/posing_questions.pdf

*Geography Students Interview Faculty About Their Research*
At University College London, United Kingdom, eleven year-one students do an assignment in term one in which students interview a member of faculty about their research. Each first-year tutorial group is allocated a member of faculty who is not their tutor. Tutorial groups are given by that member of faculty three pieces of writing that are representative of their work, along with their CV, and arrange a date for the interview. Before the interview, students read these materials and develop an interview schedule (protocol). On the basis of their reading and the interview, each student individually writes a 1,500 word report on the objectives of the interviewee's research; how that research relates to their earlier studies; and how the interviewee's research relates to his or her teaching, other interests, and geography as a whole.
Source: Dwyer (2001)

*Engaging Students in Community-Based Projects*
In the Arts of Citizenship Program at the University of Michigan in the United States, students combine learning and research with practical projects that enhance community life. For example, in the Underground Railroad project, they collaborated with the African American Cultural and Historical Museum of Washtenaw County to research nineteenth-century antislavery activism and African American community life in the area and then displayed the historical exhibit, "Midnight Journey," to more than twenty thousand people at schools, libraries, and museums in Michigan and Ontario.
www.artsofcitizenship.umich.edu/about/program.html

*Inquiry in the Humanities*
The Level-1 course, Inquiry in the Humanities, is part of a university-wide project on inquiry-based learning at McMaster University, Canada. In the humanities the course introduces first-year students to the research environment through small sections, group discussions, and workshops, which complement the emphasis in the humanities on developing articulate oral and written skills.
http://www.humanities.mcmaster.ca/LevOne/courses/inquiry.html

*History Students Contribute Research Findings to a Web Site*
At the University of Victoria, British Columbia, Canada, History 481: Micro History and the Internet is a learner-centered and research-oriented course in which the main activity is primary archival research on various aspects of life in Victoria, British Columbia, from 1843 to 1900. Students work in small groups to conduct the research and eventually to publish their findings on the Web site called "Victoria's Victoria," which was launched at the end of the first delivery of the course in 2002.
http://web.uvic.ca/terc/newletter/documents/sept_03_newsletter.pdf; http://web.uvic.ca/vv/

A key feature in all these examples is that students are actively engaged in constructing, interpreting, or disseminating knowledge. Such a learning-by-doing approach is an effective way for students to benefit from faculty research (Gibbs, 1988; Healey and Roberts, 2004). For example, Baxter

Magolda (1999) found that students engaged in research-based learning develop more sophisticated levels of intellectual development. She sees such research as "constructive development pedagogy . . . [in which] teachers model the process of constructing knowledge in their disciplines, teach that process to students, and give students opportunities to practice and become proficient at it" (p. 9).

## Recognize Roles of Course Teams, Departments, and Institutions

Many of the suggestions presented to this point have been developed by individual faculty. However, some of the suggestions require the resources and cooperation of groups of faculty and often institutional or even national funding and organization (see Chapter Two in this volume). All will have more impact if they are part of a coherent design by the course team to ensure that all students are supported and required to develop an understanding of and through research. In looking at an overall student degree program, the metaquestions one should ask include the following:

- How do introductory courses introduce students to the complexities of knowledge in their disciplines?
- How does the overall program develop this initial understanding, equip them with the research methodologies appropriate to their context, and provide a range of opportunities for them to investigate particular issues?
- How does the program ensure that all or selected students have an opportunity for an extended research experience or a capstone course that supports their understanding of knowledge complexity in their discipline(s)?

The Boyer Commission on Educating Undergraduates in the Research University (1998) suggests that such research-based learning should be standard and that it should begin with inquiry-based learning in year one and end with a capstone experience based around a major project. A different approach, and a rare example of institution-wide curriculum development, is provided by Roskilde University, Denmark. Interdisciplinary group projects count for half of the assessment in the first and second years; in the next two years students undertake projects in each of the two disciplines they study, and the extent to which these projects are integrated is left to them (Legge, 1997).

To develop coherent curricula requires course teams and departments to take a proactive approach to organizing the resources available, in particular to capitalize on the faculty's diverse roles and talents. A range of questions departments can ask of themselves to ensure that effective teaching-research links are developed is given in Jenkins and Zetter (2003, p. 19).

NEW DIRECTIONS FOR TEACHING AND LEARNING • DOI: 10.1002/tl

## In Conclusion: This Is But One Approach, But the Key One!

In presenting this approach to course design, whether by individuals, course teams, or departments, we recognize that ensuring teaching-research links is but one aspect that needs to be considered in designing courses. Jenkins (1998) has likened designing courses to controlling a Ouija board, where the curriculum is shaped by a variety of forces, including the overall resources available; the university regulations and requirements, such as the time allotted to a course (module); the need and pressures to support student employability, lifelong learning, and preparation for civic roles; and as we have argued here, the shaping of teaching-research links. Our focus on supporting teaching-research links is partly for reasons of faculty and student motivation, but ultimately because the teaching-research nexus should be what distinguishes higher education from high school or vocational education. An important aim of higher education is to support students to realize not only the contested uncertain nature of knowledge, but also the importance and the fascination of pursuing that knowledge. Some would argue that this ideal is not only critical for ensuring that what the students experience is higher education; it is also important for subsequent employability. Thus Scott (2002, p. 13) has argued, "We are all researchers now. . . . Teaching and research are becoming ever more intimately related. . . . In a 'knowledge society' all students—certainly all graduates—have to be researchers. Not only are they engaged in the production of knowledge; they must also be educated to cope with the risks and uncertainties generated by the advance of science."

In achieving or getting as close as possible to that ideal, the key issue in linking teaching and research is how we design, deliver, evaluate, and grade (assess) appropriate research or inquiry-based learning courses for *all* students in higher education.

## References

Barnett, R. *Realizing the University in an Age of Supercomplexity.* Maidenhead, United Kingdom: Society for Research into Higher Education and Open University Press, 2000.

Baxter Magolda, M. B. *Creating Contexts for Learning and Self-Authorship: Constructive-Developmental Pedagogy.* Nashville, Tenn.: Vanderbilt University Press, 1999.

Becher, T., and Trowler, P. R. *Academic Tribes and Territories: Intellectual Inquiry and the Cultures of Disciplines.* (2nd ed.) Maidenhead, United Kingdom: Society for Research into Higher Education and Open University Press, 2001.

Biglan, A. "The Characteristics of Subject Matter in Different Scientific Areas." *Journal of Applied Psychology,* 1973, 57(3), 195–203.

Boyer Commission on Educating Undergraduates in the Research University. *Reinventing Undergraduate Education: A Blueprint for America's Research Universities.* Stony Brook: State University of New York, 1998.

Dwyer, C. "Linking Research and Teaching: A Staff-Student Interview Project." *Journal of Geography in Higher Education,* 2001, *25*(3), 357–366.

Elton, L. "Scholarship and the Research and Teaching Nexus." In R. Barnett (ed.), *Reshaping the University: New Relationships Between Research, Scholarship and Teaching.* Maidenhead, United Kingdom: Open University Press, 2005.

Gibbs, G. *Learning by Doing: A Guide to Teaching and Learning Methods.* London: Further Education Unit, 1988. http://www.glos.ac.uk/gdn/gibbs/index.htm. Accessed Aug. 2, 2006.

Griffiths, R. "Knowledge Production and the Research-Teaching Nexus: The Case of the Built Environment Disciplines." *Studies in Higher Education,* 2004, *29*(6), 709–726.

Healey, M. "Linking Research and Teaching: Exploring Disciplinary Spaces and the Role of Inquiry-Based Learning." In R. Barnett (ed.), *Reshaping the University: New Relationships Between Research, Scholarship and Teaching.* Maidenhead, United Kingdom: Open University Press, 2005a.

Healey, M. "Linking Research and Teaching to Benefit Student Learning." *Journal of Geography in Higher Education,* 2005b, *29*(2), 183–201.

Healey, M., and Jenkins, A. "Discipline-Based Educational Development." In H. Eggins and R. Macdonald (eds.), *The Scholarship of Academic Development.* Maidenhead, United Kingdom: Society for Research into Higher Education and Open University Press, 2003.

Healey, M., Jenkins, A., and Kneale, P. "Small Worlds on an Interconnected Planet: Teaching and Learning Geography in Higher Education." In C. Rust (ed.), *Improving Student Learning Through the Disciplines.* Oxford: Oxford Center for Staff and Learning Development, Oxford Brookes University, 2000.

Healey, M., Jordan, F., Pell, B., and Short, C. "The Research-Teaching Nexus: Student Experiences of Research and Consultancy." Unpublished manuscript, n.d.

Healey, M., and Roberts, J. (eds.). *Engaging Students in Active Learning: Case Studies in Geography, Environment and Related Disciplines.* Cheltenham: Geography Discipline Network and School of Environment, University of Gloucestershire, 2004. http://www.glos.ac.uk/gdn/active/student.htm. Accessed Aug. 2, 2005.

Jenkins, A. *Curriculum Design in Geography.* Cheltenham: Geography Discipline Network, University of Gloucestershire, 1998.

Jenkins, A. *A Guide to the Research Evidence on Teaching-Research Relationships.* York, United Kingdom: Higher Education Academy, 2004. http://www.heacademy.ac.uk/embedded_object.asp?id=21570&file. Accessed Aug. 2, 2006.

Jenkins, A., Blackman, T., Lindsay, R., and Paton-Saltzberg, R. "Teaching and Research: Student Perspectives and Policy Implications." *Studies in Higher Education,* 1998, *23*(2), 127–141.

Jenkins, A., Breen, R., and Lindsay, R., with Brew, A. *Re-Shaping Higher Education: Linking Teaching and Research.* London: SEDA and Routledge, 2003.

Jenkins, A., and Healey, M. *Institutional Strategies to Link Teaching and Research.* York, United Kingdom: Higher Education Academy, 2005. http://www.heacademy.ac.uk/resources.asp?process=full_record&section=generic&id=585. Accessed Aug. 2, 2006.

Jenkins, A., and Zetter, R. *Linking Teaching and Research in Departments.* York: Higher Education Academy, 2003. http://www.heacademy.ac.uk/embedded_object.asp?id=18633&file. Accessed Aug. 2, 2006.

Kinkead, J. (ed.). *Valuing and Supporting Undergraduate Research.* New Directions for Teaching and Learning, no. 93. San Francisco: Jossey-Bass, 2003.

Legge, K. *Problem-Orientated Group Project Work at Roskilde University.* Roskilde, Denmark: Roskilde University Press, 1997.

NEW DIRECTIONS FOR TEACHING AND LEARNING • DOI: 10.1002/tl

Scott, P. "High Wire: We Are All Researchers Now." *Guardian Education,* Jan. 28, 2002, p. 13.
Zamorski, B. "Research-Led Teaching and Learning in Higher Education: A Case." *Teaching in Higher Education,* 2002, 7(4), 411–427.

*MICK HEALEY, professor of geography at the University of Gloucestershire, United Kingdom, was awarded one of the first National Teaching Fellowships in 2000. He is codirector of the Center for Active Learning in Geography, Environment and Related Disciplines.*

*ALAN JENKINS is Reinvention Fellow of the Reinvention Center for Undergraduate Research at the Universities of Warwick and Oxford Brookes. He is an associate practitioner for the United Kingdom Higher Education Academy.*

# 6

*Our role as teachers in universities should not be to simply keep up-to-date with new technologies; rather, we should be leaders in the use of new and emerging technologies to effectively meet the changing needs of learners.*

# Inquiry-Based Learning with the Net: Opportunities and Challenges

*Heather Kanuka*

> I believe that the main hope for realizing a genuinely student centered undergraduate education lies in re-engineering the teaching-research nexus.
>
> Paul Ramsden (2001)

A defining attribute of a university is that its academic members are both active researchers and teachers. Ideally, the roles of teacher and researcher will coexist in a mutually reinforcing and recursive relationship (Braxton, 1996; Crittenden, 1997; Harrison, 2002). In theory, the unique research-teaching link can enlighten, inspire, and enrich the other in a symbiotic relationship. Students learn and are motivated by an environment of inquiry, while academics are stimulated and enthused by the act of teaching and interacting with their students. And although there may be little empirical evidence to support the notion that this kind of teaching-research connection exists (Marsh and Hattie, 2002), as Healey and Jenkins point out in Chapter Five of this volume, this is nevertheless what distinguishes universities from other vocational and postsecondary institutions. It follows, then, that at the heart of a meaningful education in universities should be a commitment to the development of the teaching-research link and instilling a sense of inquiry in our students through research with inquiry-based learning approaches.

Supporters of inquiry-based learning argue that outcomes of this approach include higher-order learning, often identified as critical thinking, self-directed and self-regulated learning, and learning how to learn—or metacognition. Theorists of educational technology have argued further that the Internet (or simply, the Net) is an excellent educational resource that can be used to facilitate inquiry-based learning and the development of higher-order learning skills.

## Inquiry-Based Learning and the Net: What's the Link?

Understanding inquiry-based learning with the Net involves recognizing that learning using the Net is fundamentally different from learning with other kinds of educational technologies (such as interactive video, computer-assisted learning, CD-ROM encyclopedias or tutorials, microworlds, or electronic databases). What characterizes the Net as a unique tool for inquiry-based learning is its hypertext-linking structure. The basic assumption behind the effectiveness of hypertext linking for inquiry-based learning is its ability to change text from a traditional linear structure to one that more closely mimics learners' cognitive structures as they are constructing knowledge (Spiro and Feltovich, 1991).

*Hypertext* is a term coined by Nelson (1967) for a collection of documents or "nodes." The hypertext concept, in turn, has been used by several developers of the Internet. Nelson's vision of hypertext involved implementation of a *docuverse,* where information is stored on a node and accessible by a link from any other node. Navigation through the nodes is nonlinear and dependent on each individual's choice of links. This nonlinear linking idea was applied to the Net through the hypertext transfer protocol (HTTP). Although the value of using hypertext links in the learning process became evident to many teacher practitioners with the invention of the World Wide Web, educational technologists had theorized about the value of using hypertext links in the learning process shortly after Nelson's vision was introduced in 1963, with the principal benefit being cited as its ability to mimic our mental models (Kearsley, 1988; Marchionini, 1988).

Figure 6.1 illustrates how hypertext, like our minds, provides links that can jump from one thought to another based on our interests or needs.

As the figure illustrates, hypertext links not only store and manipulate information—which can be done on paper—but are also free of linear and spatial constraints. In this way, students who use hypertext links can be released from the directed and linear structure of print-based resources and can browse among Web pages, moving easily through large amounts of information in a student-directed manner that reflects their own mental models. Moreover, with print-based media (such as textbooks) it is fairly safe to assume that students most often read the information sequentially from the beginning to end. With hypertext links students have immediate access to any knowledge or information repositories moderated by the fol-

NEW DIRECTIONS FOR TEACHING AND LEARNING • DOI: 10.1002/tl

**Figure 6.1. Hypertext Links Allow Students to Jump from One Thought to Another Based on Their Interests and Needs.**

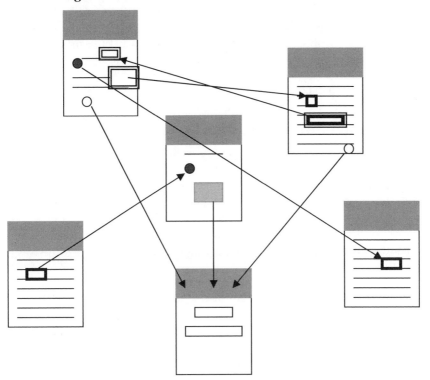

lowing variables or characteristics: personal relevance, interest level, experience, information needs, and task demands (Jonassen, 1988).

Thus the Net allows instructors to present a large amount of information in a way that invites students to make their own decisions about which links to follow and which not to, thereby giving them greater control of their learning. The result can be an enhancement of thinking skills, such as metacognition. Our ability to "metacognitize" has been associated with higher-order thinking and involves active control over the cognitive processes. Learner-controlled activities, such as planning how to approach a given learning task, monitoring understanding, and evaluating progress toward achievement of tasks, are metacognitive in nature. Irrespective of how a Web site is designed, it is at the students' discretion whether or not a sequence is followed and whether a link is accessed.

The use of the Net for inquiry-based learning, then, necessitates that students continually make decisions about which links to follow and to assess their state of progress (Roselli, 1991). Educational-technology theorists have maintained that the constant decision making and self-directed evaluation of progress forces students to apply higher-order intellectual skills. Few would disagree with Garrison and Archer (2000), who maintain that the aim of higher education is to develop the thinking and learning abilities of students, which is achieved when students actively direct their own learning and develop meaningful knowledge structures on the basis of their experiences. Underpinning this assertion is the assumption that students will assume responsibility for their learning and by default, instructors will relinquish control of the learning activities to the students.

## Learner Control Versus Learner Chaos

There are, however, a few shortcomings when instructors relinquish control and let learners roam the Net. Inquiry-based learning using the Net with high levels of learner control and hypertext links can provide students with the freedom that can enhance and enrich the learning experience, but it can also create chaos and confusion. Simply providing students with access to the Net does not automatically promote effective inquiry-based learning. The three most commonly cited problems using the Net without carefully designed instructional strategies include lack of logical organization of information, enticing Web sites that rob learners of their time, and questionable reliability and credibility of information (Quinlan, 1997).

Understanding the effects of learner control necessitates understanding the Net on two levels: technology and learning. The prime technical issue is the seemingly endless amounts of information that students can link to. The process of accessing information involves students making decisions about which, if any, hypertext link(s) to follow. That is, learners can decide whether to choose paths identified by explicit connections or to navigate freely in tune with their individual capacity and aims. Consequently, hypertext can create inquiry-based learning environments endowed with high quantities of information for research on any topic but it may also lead to serious problems precisely due to the amount of information that can be freely accessed (Marchionini, 1988; Roselli, 1991). For example, accessing numerous Web sites can result in learner disorientation or cognitive overload. Cognitive overload can then give rise to a further problem called *conceptual disorientation* that occurs when a student loses sight of the task while exploring on the Net. Some students have described this experience as chaotic, unstructured, and even somewhat frightening (Berenfeld, 1996).

The broad concept of learner control, whereby the onus of responsibility for directing the learning activities rests with the student, has been well researched. The results have revealed with consistency that under certain circumstances there are negative consequences when students are provided with high degrees of learner control (Steinberg, 1991). This research provides important insights into how to address the challenges of using the Net to facilitate inquiry-based learning.

Early research on learner control (prior to the 1980s) tended to focus on control of course flow, control of structural features of instruction, and motivational effects of learner control (Steinberg, 1989). The results of these studies showed that some learners' achievement was the same with control as without control—but learners who were poor performers in the subject area learned the least. These learners seemed to have two characteristics in common: they failed to employ adequate review strategies, and they did not know how to manage their time and thus frequently did not complete the course during the allotted time.

As a whole, the outcomes of early research on learner control indicate, first, that students learn less with high levels of learner control and are not very proficient at selecting exercises at appropriate difficulty levels, and second, that students who are high achievers in the subject area are most likely to manage their learning appropriately. Third, this research reveals that at times high degrees of learner control result in greater task engagement and better attitudes but not necessarily in greater achievement—and at times can even lead to worse performance (Steinberg, 1989). Further research on learner control exploring the relationships between aptitude and personality traits also yielded no definitive conclusions. Moreover, while many students are motivated by learner control, others are indifferent to it. These early studies were often criticized for failing to show any advantages of learner control because they did not account for the psychological processes in learning and for individual differences in learning skills and strategies. More recent research focusing on these issues revealed that the results are still in agreement with the earlier research (Eklund, 1996; Shapiro and Niederhauser, 2004; Steinberg, 1991). In general, the research indicates that when a task is easy, there are likely to be few, if any, benefits of learner control, and students with little knowledge of the content do not perform as well under high levels of learner control. Hence, the less a learner knows about a subject, the greater her or his need for instructional support.

Other researchers have studied relationships between learning outcomes and hypertext navigational paths (Misanchuck and Schwier, 1992). This research indicates that there is a relationship between high achievers and productive navigational paths chosen (Eklund, 1996). The research on student navigation also shows that students tend to adopt a structured and linear pattern similar to that taken with a book (Messing, 1990) (which is contrary to theorists claims that hypertext links on the Net provide higher-order learning because the ill-structured and non-linear learning environment mimics a learner's mental model). Other studies have shown that knowledge of the subject matter correlates highly with the ability to navigate in a nonlinear environment (Ohlsson, 1992; Alexander, Kulikowich, and Jetton, 1994). In addition, knowledge of hypertext environments predicts a greater use of the students' ability to navigate (Eklund, 1996).

These studies provide disconcerting evidence that when students are using the Net for inquiry-based learning activities in ways that provide high levels of learner control, serious problems may result. There is little doubt that access to the vast resources on the Net can effectively facilitate inquiry-based learning, especially by supporting students' knowledge structures, which are based on each student's unique set of experiences and abilities. The Net can also support the ways that students prefer to access, interact with, and interrelate with information—all of which require a high level of learner control. Unfortunately, these benefits are most likely to be realized only with learners who are high achievers, have prior knowledge of the content, and know how to navigate in a nonlinear and ill-structured environment. Failure to understand these problems when using the Net for inquiry-based learning may result in students randomly traveling through the Net experiencing ineffective and nonproductive learning.

## Using the Net for Effective Inquiry-Based Learning

Given that many students will not possess the characteristics necessary to benefit from learner-controlled, inquiry-based learning with the Net, creative instructional strategies are needed. Garrison and Archer (2000) maintain that issues of control can be resolved by using collaborative processes. Specifically, with collaborative learning, control issues can be negotiated reciprocally to be commensurate with contextual constraints and student ability. An example of a Net-based instructional strategy that effectively integrates collaborative learning is the WebQuest. This instructional strategy is in keeping with instruction that is research-based (as described by Healey and Jenkins in Chapter Five of this volume) and teaching that leads to learning in a research mode (as described by Elton in Chapter Four).

WebQuests, originally inspired by Dodge in 1995, are an inquiry-oriented activity in which information that the students use comes from the resources on the Net. WebQuests have six critical attributes: 1) an introduction to a complex problem, typically in the form of a case study; 2) engaging tasks (doable and interesting); 3) a description of the process; 4) multiple online sources and perspectives; followed by 5) evaluation; and 6) conclusions. WebQuests often also include a form of role-play as an aspect of the tasks required of the students. With respect to the design of WebQuests, most are organized in ways that require learners to work in groups. Students are divided into groups and provided with a Web document that includes a case study with an introduction and background information, as well as a group task and linked information sources that are needed to complete the task. There is a description of the process that the students should proceed through, as well as guidance on how to organize the information they acquire on the Internet. This will be followed by a conclusion that will bring closure to the group activity. The closure activity requires students to reflect on what they have learned through the case study and group activity (role-playing), followed by extending the experience to other domains.

The effectiveness of a WebQuest results, to a large extent, from the integration of case studies and role-playing. When creatively designed, case studies support a learning environment that seeks to present the complex reality of any issue with its concomitant ambiguity and multidimensionality, thus providing a strong image of the multifaceted and complex nature of most subject areas (Lacey and Merseth, 1993). The multifaceted nature of the complex problem presented in a case study is then illustrated through strategic links on the Net. The Net's hypertext linking ability (which is the defining attribute of a WebQuest) provides opportunities for students to conduct research on the complex concepts presented in the case study from multiple perspectives, for various purposes, and via different learning strategies (Lanza, 1991). Such a multidimensional approach requires careful selection of Web sites with diverse perspectives and disciplines. As students return to the same complex phenomenon from different perspectives, they experience the diversity of uses of ill-structured knowledge and may recognize patterns of multiple interconnectedness and context dependency of concepts as they navigate among knowledge domains using hypertext links. Consequently, the strategy encourages them to reflect on complex knowledge from many different perspectives (Spiro and Feltovitch, 1991).

The primary purpose of role-playing in a WebQuest is to offer students the ability to practice the unfamiliar in a safe environment and acquire a variety of contradictory viewpoints. Role-playing can provide an opportunity to expose learners to a variety of perspectives by asking them to assume the role of others with different viewpoints (Renner, 1999). According to Hiltz and Turoff (1978), role-playing is one of the most promising instructional methods for text-based Internet communication technologies. Specifically, role-playing can be done more authentically through text-based computer conferencing than in some of the face-to-face activities, especially if the students are not able to tell who the other players are. Collett, Kanuka, Blanchette, and Goodale (1999) also note that role-playing may be more effective with computer conferencing because learners are frequently uncomfortable when asked to assume a role in front of their peers. Physical characteristics can also be difficult to overcome in that participants and observers may find they relate to the real person rather than the character being portrayed. When conducted using computer conferencing, students can be provided with pseudonyms (or alias e-mails) so that everyone knows each other only as the characters they have been asked to portray. This temporary anonymity not only helps students to play their roles more convincingly, but also helps them, through their assigned roles, to acquire an understanding of others' worldviews.

Research on WebQuests has shown, with surprising consistency, that they are effective both in terms of student satisfaction and achieving high levels of learning (Kanuka, Rourke, and Laflamme, forthcoming; McGlinn and McGlinn, 2003; Thomas, 1998). In particular, research has demonstrated that the case studies used in WebQuests can be very effective as an introduction to a complex scenario, while the role-playing requires the students to be collaborative, active, and interactive through debate and discussion, understand their peers' points of view, and articulate their own. There is also evidence that the role-playing motivates students to seek out relevant information to support their assigned role and provide solutions to the case presented. Finally, unlike other collaborative group activities, research has shown that WebQuests tend to eliminate issues of uneven workloads among group participants (Kanuka, 2005).

Thus, the use of case studies, in combination with the role-playing and access to hypertext links within the WebQuest activity, can facilitate the development of deeper and more meaningful understandings. Nevertheless, perhaps the most likely reason for the success of WebQuests in facilitating higher-order learning is that WebQuests provide structured access to the resources available on the Net while encouraging a spirit of inquiry. This kind of planned, inquiry-based learning activity motivates students to engage in guided exploration from multiple perspectives and results in the development of sophisticated and diverse understandings. It is also an excellent way to gain the most from the unique properties of the Net. Examples of WebQuests developed for learning in higher education can be found at http://webquest.org/.

## References

Alexander, P. A., Kulikowich, J. M., and Jetton, T. L. "The Role of Subject-Matter Knowledge and Interest in Processing of Linear and Nonlinear Texts." *Review of Educational Research*, 1994, 64(2), 201–252.

Berenfeld, B. "Linking Students to the Infosphere." *T.H.E. Journal*, 1996, 23, 76–83.

Braxton, J. M. (ed.). *Contrasting Perspectives on the Relationship Between Teaching and Research.* New Directions for Institutional Research, no. 2. San Francisco: Jossey-Bass, 1996.

Collett, D., Kanuka, H., Blanchette, J., and Goodale, C. *Learning Technologies in Adult Distance Education.* Edmonton: University of Alberta, 1999.

Crittenden, B. *Minding Their Business: The Proper Role of Universities and Some Suggested Reforms.* Canberra, Australian Capital Territory: Academy of the Social Sciences, 1997.

Dodge, B. *Some Thoughts About WebQuests.* 1995. http://edWeb.sdsu.edu/courses/edtec596/about_Webquests.html. Accessed Jan. 12, 2006.

Eklund, J. "Cognitive Models for Structuring Hypermedia and Implications for Learning from the World Wide Web." In *Proceedings of AusWeb.* 1996. http://ausweb.scu.edu.au/aw95/hypertext/eklund/. Accessed Jan. 12, 2006.

Garrison, D. R., and Archer, W. *A Transactional Perspective on Teaching and Learning. A Framework for Adult and Higher Education.* New York: Pergamon, 2000.

Harrison, J. E. "The Quality of University Teaching: Faculty Performance and Accountability. A Literature Review." *CSSHE Professional File*, Spring 2002, pp. 1–18.

Hiltz, S. R., and Turoff, M. *The Networked Nation: Human Communication via Computer.* Reading, Mass.: Addison-Wesley, 1978.

Jonassen, D. H. "Designing Structured Hypertext and Structuring Access to Hypertext." *Educational Technology*, 1988, 28(11), 13–16.

Kanuka, H. "An Exploration into Facilitating Higher Levels of Learning in a Text-Based Internet Learning Environment Using Diverse Instructional Strategies." *Journal of Computer Mediated Communication,* 2005, *10*(3). http://jcmc.indiana.edu/vol10/issue3/kanuka.html. Accessed Jan. 12, 2006.

Kanuka, H., Rourke, L., and Laflamme, E. "The Influence of Instructional Methods on the Quality of Online Discussion." *British Journal of Educational Technology,* forthcoming.

Kearsley, G. P. "Authoring Considerations for Hypertext." *Educational Technology,* 1988, *28*(11), 21–24.

Lacey, C. A., and Merseth, K. K. "Cases, Hypermedia and Computer Networks: Three Curricular Innovations for Teacher Education." *Journal of Curriculum Studies,* 1993, *25*(6), 543–551.

Lanza, A. "Some Guidelines for the Design of Effective Hypercourses." *Educational Technology,* 1991, *31*(10), 18–22.

Marchionini, G. "Hypermedia and Learning: Freedom and Chaos." *Educational Technology,* 1988, *28*(11), 8–12.

McGlinn, J. E., and McGlinn, J. M. *Motivating Learning in a Humanities Class Through Innovative Research Assignments: A Case Study, 2003.* ERIC Document Reproduction Service (ED 479 392).

Messing, J. *The Use of Content and Teaching Strategy Control Features in Computer Assisted Learning Courseware, 1990.* ERIC Document Reproductive Service (ED 59246).

Misanchuck, E., and Schwier, R. "Representing Interactive Multimedia and Hypermedia Audit Trails." *Journal of Educational Multimedia and Hypermedia,* 1992, *11*(3), 355–372.

Nelson, T. H. "Getting It Out of Our System." In G. Schechter (ed.), *Information Retrieval: A Critical Review.* Washington, D.C.: Thompson, 1967.

Ohlsson, S. "The Interaction Between Knowledge and Practice in the Acquisition of Cognitive Skills." In A. Meyrowitz and S. Chipman (eds.), *Foundations of Knowledge Acquisition: Cognitive Models of Complex Learning.* Norwell, Mass.: Kluwer, 1992.

Quinlan, L. A. "Creating a Classroom Kaleidoscope with the World Wide Web." *Educational Technology,* 1997, *37*(3), 15–22.

Renner, P. *The Art of Teaching Adults: How to Become an Exceptional Instructor and Facilitator.* Vancouver, B.C.: Training Associates, 1999.

Roselli, T. "Control of User Disorientation in Hypertext Systems." *Educational Technology,* 1991, *31*(12), 42–46.

Shapiro, A., and Niederhauser, D. "Learning from Hypertext: Research Issues and Findings." In D. H. Jonassen (ed.), *Handbook of Research for Educational Communications and Technology.* (2nd ed.). Mahwah, N.J.: Erlbaum, 2004.

Spiro, R. J., and Feltovich, P. J. "Cognitive Flexibility, Constructivism, and Hypertext: Random Access Instruction for Advanced Knowledge Acquisition in Ill-Structured Domains." *Educational Technology,* 1991, *31,* 24–33.

Steinberg, E. R. "Cognition and Learner Control: A Literature Review, 1977–1988." *Journal of Computer-Based Instruction,* 1989, *16*(4), 117–121.

Steinberg, E. R. *Computer-Assisted Instruction: A Synthesis of Theory, Practice, and Technology.* Mahwah, N.J.: Erlbaum, 1991.

Thomas, A. *The Interactive, Virtual Management Information Systems (MIS) Classroom: Creating an Active Learning Environment on the Internet, 1998.* ERIC Document Reproduction Service (ED 427682).

HEATHER KANUKA *is a Canada Research Chair and associate professor at Athabasca University, Canada.*

# PART THREE

Research-Based Teaching as
Pedagogical Inquiry

*7*

*The disciplines contribute in a variety of ways to inquiry-based learning about teaching but they also can be seen as the beneficiaries of such pedagogical work.*

# Disciplines, Pedagogy, and Inquiry-Based Learning About Teaching

*Mary Taylor Huber*

Some years ago, at a conference on the scholarship of teaching and learning in London, I was asked to speak about "Disciplinary Styles in the Scholarship of Teaching and Learning," the topic and title of a collection of essays that had recently been published in the United States (Huber and Morreale, 2002a). I argued that when faculty members begin to look seriously at their own teaching and their own students' learning, they bring their disciplines' intellectual styles and resources to the task. Indeed, I continued, when these same faculty members come together with people from other disciplines, they often find attractive concepts and useful methods from neighboring (and even distant) fields to borrow and adapt for the study and solution of pedagogical problems in their own disciplinary contexts.

When the question-and-answer session began, the first hand up was from a distinguished senior scholar of higher education. "What about theory," he thundered, "and all the existing research on student learning and faculty development?" His view, apparently shared by many in these fields, was that faculty members should be attending first, and with some urgency, to work focused on teaching and learning by educationists, psychologists, and others in the learning sciences.

This exchange, so baldly laid out, invites the obvious riposte that when it comes to improving teaching, everything should be fair game. I was not suggesting that faculty members ignore cross-cutting work, like Bloom's classifications of learning (1956), Perry's stages of intellectual development (1998), or the U.S. National Research Council's recent report

New Directions for Teaching and Learning, no. 107, Fall 2006 © Wiley Periodicals, Inc.
Published online in Wiley InterScience (www.interscience.wiley.com) • DOI: 10.1002/tl.245

on what scientists are finding out about how people learn (Bransford, Brown, and Cocking, 1999). Nor do I think that my interlocutor was suggesting that "generic" theory is the only body of work that could or should inform pedagogical practice. Still, while the extremes are clearly untenable, our conversation in London does point to a continuing tension in the scholarship of teaching and learning community about the nature and value of what the academic disciplines (other than education and the learning sciences) can contribute to the enterprise.

In this essay, I explore three reasons for taking the disciplines very seriously. First, and most important, the disciplines offer a *way in* to the scholarship of teaching and learning (which in this chapter I use synonymously with inquiry-based learning about teaching), through faculty members' concern for what and how well students are learning these fields. Second, more controversially, the disciplines offer college faculty a *way to do* the scholarship of teaching and learning through the intellectual skills and resources they have access to as members of their particular professional communities. Finally, and more speculatively, I suggest that because knowledge practices are changing in many disciplines today, this may be an opportune time for the development in them of a more reflective, even critical, pedagogy that could reconfigure expectations for what—and how—people teach and learn in those fields. Indeed, I end by suggesting that we may wish to shift the question from what the disciplines can contribute to inquiry-based learning about teaching (or the scholarship of teaching and learning), and ask what pedagogical work that is deeply informed by its disciplinary context can give back to the discipline itself.

## Disciplinary Ways in the Scholarship of Teaching and Learning

Most college and university teachers hold their highest degree in the discipline that they teach, and most remain members of that scholarly community throughout their careers. This identity affects nearly every aspect of their academic lives: what they read, the research they do, the conferences they attend, where they are located on campus, even how they decorate their offices—and of course, the who, what, where, when, how, and why of their teaching (Becher and Trowler, 2001). Most faculty members have learned much of what they know about teaching and learning from their own experience as students and from colleagues in their own fields, and most are familiar with their own discipline's traditional repertoire of pedagogies (lectures, seminars, labs, fieldwork, problem sets, and so forth) as well as with more recent debates (such as calculus reform in mathematics; the literary canon in English), and developments (such as online archives in the humanities) that bear on the teaching of those fields.

This is not to say that the disciplines are the only communities that affect teachers' pedagogical goals and imaginations. Certainly, in United

States colleges and universities, disciplinary faculty members are likely also to see themselves as participants in a larger project of liberal or professional education, which might involve teaching first-year seminars on interdisciplinary themes or redesigning disciplinary courses to align with institutional goals for writing, critical thinking, or quantitative literacy. Some, motivated by commitment to a civic role for higher education, might introduce a service-learning component to their courses; early adopters across the disciplinary spectrum might experiment with new ways of using technology. Some teachers will be intrigued by pedagogies in other fields, like the chemist at the University of Michigan whose design for an honors program involving peer instruction drew on his own experience in undergraduate studio courses in the arts (Coppola, Ege, and Lawton, 1997). Others will try classroom assessment or collaborative learning techniques that they've practiced in workshops sponsored by their institution's teaching and learning center. Indeed, with the development of a teaching commons in higher education, previously unconnected pedagogical conversations are connecting so that cross-fertilization between the disciplines is more likely to take place (Huber and Hutchings, 2005).

Although this teaching commons greatly enriches the range of resources available to college and university teachers, it does not diminish the importance of the disciplines as ways in to pedagogical reflection more generally, and especially to the scholarship of teaching and learning. As Bass (1999) notes in a much-cited essay, the necessary first step is for faculty members to experience classroom "problems" not as indicators of something shameful or bad about themselves or their students, but as invitations to inquiry and innovation. For many (most?) scholars of teaching and learning so far, the home discipline is where classroom problems with the requisite intellectual depth and moral force have been most likely to arise.

This situation should not be surprising. The disciplines (or at least closely related groups of them) vary considerably in regard to which arts of intellectualizing are most salient to their particular agendas and problem-solving styles (Donald, 2002). This variation means that mathematics faculty members are likely to encounter a different set of teaching problems than those in chemistry, engineering, sociology, literature, history, or music. And figuring out what these problems are really about can be exciting, because it brings teachers face to face with what they, as experts, have learned to take for granted and what their students, as novices, generally do not (see Langer, 1992; Riordan and Roth, 2005; Mills and Huber, 2005). Whether it is the odd nature of the meaning of "proof" in mathematics or the special role of difficulty in understanding a poem, the problems students have in learning a field can be keys to imagining alternative ways to help more than just A-students "get it" and begin a meaningful engagement with the discipline's most basic orientations to subject matter, method, and the world (see Graff, 2003). As Riordan argues: "Creating ways to make a discipline come alive for those who are not experts requires rigorous thought about what really matters in a field and how to engage students in its practice" (2005, p. xii).

Although many faculty members arrive at these insights more or less on their own through a gradual intensification of their teaching interests and educational concerns, a number of programs aimed at fostering the scholarship of teaching and learning take advantage of teachers' disciplinary engagements and expertise (Jenkins, 1996; Healey, 2002; Wright, 2003). For example, the Indiana University program described by Middendorf and Pace in *Decoding the Disciplines: Helping Students Learn Disciplinary Ways of Thinking* (2004) leads participants through a set of seven questions aimed at piquing their curiosity and engaging them deeply with the pedagogy of their own fields: "What is a bottleneck to learning in this class? How does an expert do these things? How can these tasks be explicitly modeled? How will students practice these skills and get feedback? What will motivate the students? How well are students mastering these learning tasks? How can the resulting knowledge about learning be shared?" (Clearly, such lessons are also useful for students themselves, as Pace and Pugh (1996) show in *Studying for History*—one of a series for students about studying different disciplines.)

## Disciplinary Ways to Do the Scholarship of Teaching and Learning

It is one thing to acknowledge that faculty members' various disciplinary interests and commitments offer productive ways in to the scholarship of teaching and learning, but quite another to suggest that the various disciplines offer ways to do it as well. After all, questioning is only the first step. As Hutchings and I note, once faculty members "begin to think of teaching as a source of challenging, intellectual questions, a second imperative emerges: to devise ways to explore those questions and shed light on them. The scholarship of teaching and learning is not simply a casual interlude of mulling and reflection. Though it may be of limited scope and scale, and therefore modest in one sense, it entails systematic, disciplined inquiry, and requires hard thinking about how to gather and analyze evidence" (Huber and Hutchings, 2005, pp. 23–24).

Clearly, "disciplined inquiry" invites the use of a faculty member's disciplinary imagination. This may be seen in the style a scholar chooses for documenting teaching and learning in a course portfolio, in the kind of conceptual framing a scholar may use to develop and present learning goals for a lesson or a course, and most obviously, in the methods a scholar may adapt for empirical study. Yet herein lies a challenge. The scholarship of teaching and learning is typically pursued as a kind of practitioner or action research by teachers in their own classrooms, not the circumstances or settings for which the investigative methods used in most disciplines— including education and the learning sciences—are well designed. Doing the scholarship of teaching and learning sits, therefore, at the edge of most disciplines, calling on but also going beyond the normal knowledge practices of most fields (Huber, 2000).

At the most fundamental level, that of understanding the necessity and nature of inquiry itself, academics do bring useful intellectual capital, habits of mind, and modes of collaboration that they have developed as professional scholars in their fields. For many, this skill set includes familiarity with literature that can be tapped in developing concepts for pedagogical work: reader-response theory in English, for example, or organizational theory in management. Scholars from fields without an obviously relevant literature at the core, like chemistry or mathematics, often cite a specific orientation to the identification and solution of problems as central to both their disciplinary and pedagogical research.

There are also organized attempts to domesticate the scholarship of teaching and learning within particular families of fields. For example, leaders of the Center for the Integration of Research, Teaching, and Learning in Wisconsin have been quite inventive in using practices from the research cultures of the sciences to scaffold pedagogical inquiry for graduate students in these fields. These practices include encouraging students to treat teaching as research by using a scientific paradigm involving hypothesis, experiment, observation, analysis, and improvement; experimenting with the disciplinary seminar, in which a mixed community of professors, postdoctoral, and doctoral students discuss a small piece of pedagogical research; and modeling mentorship for teaching on a pattern with which doctoral students are familiar—the laboratory director (Mathieu, 2004).

Indeed, when designing classroom inquiry projects in the scholarship of teaching and learning, many faculty members do choose methods that reflect or resonate with the traditions of investigation in their own fields. In the sciences and harder social sciences, the first choice is likely to be a quasi-experimental design using instruments that yield numerical results about, for example, the efficacy of this or that teaching innovation on various dimensions of student learning. Scholars in the softer social sciences or harder humanities, more comfortable with qualitative data, have, for example, found discourse analysis a useful way of exploring the dynamics of seminar participation, or tried focus groups to help understand what materials helped students negotiate the emotionally charged issues they confronted in their gender course. Others—often in fields centered on textual interpretation, where the word data is not a professional term of art—have pursued systematic inquiry through strategically designed assignments and a close reading of student work. (For examples, see Hutchings, 2000; Huber and Hutchings, 2005).

Pragmatism necessarily prevails in this enterprise, however, and people from all disciplinary backgrounds have responded to the exigencies of doing classroom research by going conceptually, methodologically, and collaboratively where they might not have gone before. In the end, for most who try it out, engaging in the scholarship of teaching and learning entails entering a cross-disciplinary "trading zone" (Huber and Morreale, 2002b) where one finds and experiments with what's on offer from other fields. This is where most scholars of teaching and learning discover the classic literature from education; techniques they can adapt, like cognitive psychology's think-aloud protocol for investigating how experts and novices go about a task; and reports on new work in the learning sciences. Yet the transactions are not only between "education" writ large and the disciplines. This is a zone in which mathematicians are enriching their own understanding of how to interpret student "errors" by adapting the idea of difficulty in literary interpretation from people in English studies, where a chemist is trying out ethnographic observation, and where a microbiologist and a communications scholar are collaborating in a study of presence in online class environments. Indeed, so great are the pleasures of interacting with others engaged in serious pedagogical reflection and research that it can become something of a burden to return to one's disciplinary home to report on the journey and recruit others to join in.

## The Disciplines as Beneficiaries of the Scholarship of Teaching and Learning

The situation of scholars of teaching and learning with regard to their own discipline is not unlike that of scholars in other cross-disciplinary endeavors who find new colleagues and new forums for sharing and building on each others' work. Yet even as the teaching commons grows and develops its own infrastructure of cross-disciplinary conferences, journals, and the like, there is growing support for pedagogical discourse in the disciplines themselves. In the United Kingdom, disciplinary conversations have been facilitated by the Higher Education Academy's network of twenty-four government-funded subject centers, each serving small sets of related disciplines. In the United States, subject-specific developments tend to be in the hands of member-funded disciplinary associations, so that getting air and column space at the associations' conferences, journals, and Web site depends on the initiative and persuasive powers of pedagogically inclined colleagues and society staff. That they are succeeding is testimony to the difficulty and complexity of college and university teaching today, its increasing visibility through a growing array of accountability initiatives, and a genuine concern among faculty members to educate students better for the challenges of personal, professional, and civic life in the twenty-first century.

No doubt the principal appeal of pedagogical conversations in most disciplinary forums is academics' desire to educate students better in their particular fields. But the disciplines can also be beneficiaries of this work through its capacity to focus attention on implicit knowledge and subterranean disciplinary change. Consider cultural anthropology, where over the past twenty years or more, there have been seismic shifts in the locations and subjects of ethnographic field work—including the growing number of anthropologists who are no longer going out to live among people who are disadvantaged or far away, but who are instead, as Marcus (2004) points out, doing work among knowledge-producing elites around the world in science, business, communications, medicine, religion, and the like. These shifts, Marcus argues, have occasioned profound changes in the conduct of ethnographic research, and he sees doctoral thesis advising as a critical site for articulating "norms and forms" for working in these new locations and thus as a laboratory for the reinvention of the core research methods of the field.

In fact, knowledge practices are changing in many disciplines, and therein lies a real opportunity for the scholarship of teaching and learning to contribute both to the individual's and the community's basic understandings of the field. These changes are certainly prompting important questions in graduate education. How, for example, "in this era when nearly all the sciences (and engineering) have shifted their focus to include the molecular level," as Kwiram (2006) writes, do you help future chemists gain the "broad perspective of the frontiers of the scientific enterprise" (p. 154)? Or as another chemist put it, how do you give doctoral students "the breadth and depth to cross boundaries within the field of chemistry and . . . work on the interfaces of their fields with other areas such as biology, medicine, solid state physics, and environmental science" (Breslow, 2006, p. 170)?

The challenge of involving students in cutting-edge practice is not limited to graduate education. Many college and university teachers today are also seeking ways to engage undergraduates in meaningful research (Jenkins and Healey, 2005; Healey and Jenkins, Chapter Five in this volume). And those among them who undertake the scholarship of teaching and learning may be able to articulate some of the changes in their fields that colleagues sense and do but have not actually yet figured out. Indeed, there are cases in the history of scholarship where people thinking about the challenges of teaching and learning a particular subject have made significant contributions to the theoretical base of the field itself. These include such fundamentals as the periodic table and the periodic law in chemistry, which "emerged during the course of the conscientious composition of a mundane chemistry textbook" (Schaffer, 2005, p. 25) and "close reading" and "much of what constitutes [literary] criticism in the 20th century" (Guillory, 2002, p. 167)—although, as both Schaffer and Guillory point out, the origins of such developments in pedagogy are often subsequently forgotten.

In conclusion, the scholarship of teaching and learning both draws on and disrupts normal expectations for intellectual inquiry and reflection in the various disciplines from which its practitioners come. By staying in tune with the literatures, methods, and modes of argumentation common in a particular field, scholars of teaching and learning are well situated to affect the pedagogy of their fellow historians, biologists, or engineers by speaking to them about problems they care about in forums they attend and in a language they understand. By going beyond the music of their field, through interactions with other fields and through critical inquiry and reflection on their own, scholars of teaching and learning can also enrich their home disciplines by helping to articulate these fields' long-established implicit pedagogies as well as new knowledge practices that are just now taking form.

## References

Bass, R. "The Scholarship of Teaching: What's the Problem?" *Inventio,* 1999, *1*(1), 1–9. http://www.doit.gmu.edu/Archives/feb98/randybass.htm. Accessed Dec. 6, 2005.

Becher, T., and Trowler, P. R. *Academic Tribes and Territories: Intellectual Enquiry and the Cultures of the Discipline.* (2nd ed.) Maidenhead, United Kingdom: Open University Press, 2001.

Bloom, B. S., and Associates. *The Taxonomy of Educational Objectives: Cognitive Domain.* New York: McKay, 1956.

Bransford, J. D., Brown, A. L., and Cocking, R. R. (eds.). *How People Learn: Brain, Mind, Experience, and School.* Washington, D.C.: National Academy Press, 1999.

Breslow, R. "Developing Breadth and Depth of Knowledge: The Doctorate in Chemistry." In C. Golde and G. Walker (eds.), *Envisioning the Future of Doctoral Education: Preparing Stewards of the Discipline.* San Francisco: Jossey-Bass, 2006.

Coppola, B. P., Ege, S. N., and Lawton, R. G. "The University of Michigan Undergraduate Chemistry Curriculum 2. Instructional Strategies and Assessment." *Journal of Chemical Education,* 1997, *74*(1), 84–94.

Donald, J. G. *Learning to Think: Disciplinary Perspectives.* San Francisco: Jossey-Bass, 2002.

Graff, G. *Clueless in Academe: How Schooling Obscures the Life of the Mind.* New Haven, Conn.: Yale University Press, 2003.

Guillory, J. "The Very Idea of Pedagogy." *Profession,* 2002, 164–171.

Healey, M. "Developing the Scholarship of Teaching in Higher Education: A Discipline-Based Approach." *Higher Education Research and Development,* 2002, *19*(2), 169–189.

Huber, M. T. "Disciplinary Styles in the Scholarship of Teaching and Learning: Reflections on the Carnegie Academy for the Scholarship of Teaching and Learning." In C. Rust (ed.), *Improving Student Learning: Improving Student Learning Through the Disciplines.* Oxford: Oxford Center for Staff and Learning Development, Oxford Brookes University, 2000.

Huber, M. T., and Hutchings, P. *The Advancement of Learning: Building the Teaching Commons.* San Francisco: Jossey-Bass, 2005.

Huber, M. T., and Morreale, S. P. (eds.). *Disciplinary Styles in the Scholarship of Teaching and Learning: Exploring Common Ground.* Washington, D.C.: American Association for Higher Education, 2002a.

Huber, M. T., and Morreale, S. P. "Situating the Scholarship of Teaching and Learning: A Cross-Disciplinary Conversation." In M. T. Huber and S. P. Morreale (eds.), *Disciplinary Styles in the Scholarship of Teaching and Learning.* Washington, D.C.: American Association for Higher Education, 2002b.

Hutchings, P. (ed.). *Opening Lines: Approaches to the Scholarship of Teaching and Learning.* Stanford, Calif.: Carnegie Foundation for the Advancement of Teaching, 2000.

Jenkins, A. "Discipline-Based Educational Development." *International Journal of Academic Development,* 1996, *1*(1), 50–62.

Jenkins, A., and Healey, M. *Institutional Strategies to Link Teaching and Research.* York, United Kingdom: Higher Education Academy, 2005.

Kwiram, A. L. "Time for Reform?" In C. Golde and G. Walker (eds.), *Envisioning the Future of Doctoral Education: Preparing Stewards of the Discipline.* San Francisco: Jossey-Bass, 2006.

Langer, J. "Speaking of Knowing: Conceptions of Understanding in Academic Disciplines." In A. Herrington and C. Moran (eds.), *Writing, Teaching, and Learning in the Disciplines.* New York: Modern Language Association, 1992.

Marcus, G. E. "Notes from Within a Laboratory for the Reinvention of Anthropological Method." Presentation at the Eighth Biannual Conference of the European Association of Social Anthropology, Vienna, Austria, Sept. 8–12, 2004.

Mathieu, R. D. "Teaching-as-Research: A Concept for Change at Research Universities." Presentation at the conference, Research and Teaching: Closing the Divide, Winchester, United Kingdom, Mar. 17, 2004. http://www.solent.ac.uk/ExternalUP/318/bob_mathieu_s_paper.doc. Accessed Dec. 6, 2005.

Middendorf, J., and Pace, D. "Decoding the Disciplines: A Model for Helping Students Learn Disciplinary Ways of Thinking." In D. Pace and J. Middendorf (eds.), *Decoding the Disciplines: Helping Students Learn Disciplinary Ways of Thinking.* New Directions for Teaching and Learning, no. 28. San Francisco: Jossey-Bass, 2004.

Mills, D., and Huber, M. T. "Anthropology and the Educational 'Trading Zone': Disciplinarity, Pedagogy, and Professionalism." *Arts and Humanities in Higher Education,* 2005, 4(1), 5–28.

Pace, D., and Pugh, S. L. *Studying for History.* New York: HarperCollins, 1996.

Perry, W. G., Jr. *Forms of Ethical and Intellectual Development in the College Years: A Scheme.* San Francisco: Jossey-Bass, 1998.

Riordan, T. "Introduction." In R. Riordan and J. Roth (eds.), *Disciplines as Frameworks for Student Learning: Teaching the Practice of the Disciplines.* Sterling, Va.: Stylus, 2005.

Riordan, T., and Roth, J. (eds.). *Disciplines as Frameworks for Student Learning: Teaching the Practice of the Disciplines.* Sterling, Va.: Stylus, 2005.

Schaffer, S. "Dozing at His Desk." *London Review of Books,* 2005, 34(13), 25–26.

Wright, S. "C-SAP's Approach in a Context of Change." Unpublished manuscript. Center for Learning and Teaching in Sociology, Anthropology and Politics (C-SAP), University of Birmingham, United Kingdom, Mar. 2003.

*MARY TAYLOR HUBER is a senior scholar at the Carnegie Foundation for the Advancement of Teaching in Stanford, California.*

NEW DIRECTIONS FOR TEACHING AND LEARNING • DOI: 10.1002/tl

8

*Through their own pedagogically oriented inquiry-based learning, teachers become better prepared to support an increasingly diverse student population in their learning.*

# Promoting Inquiry-Based Learning About Teaching Through Educational Development Units

*Carolin Kreber*

When those who teach choose to become engaged in inquiry-based learning about teaching, they start a process of pedagogical problem-solving and discovery. Simply put, they find out things about their teaching and their students' learning by actively seeking such knowledge. The process is not unlike the kind of learning they are used to in their discipline. Andresen (2000) suggests that for the work academics do to qualify as "scholarship," it must meet four quintessential features, one of which is that their work requires an "inquiry orientation." The other three features of scholarship are that it involves a deep knowledge base, is characterized by critical reflectivity, and is peer reviewed and made public. He argues that the scholarship of teaching can be observed when academics engage in critical scrutiny of the what, how, and why of teaching just the way they would with respect to any proposition in the field of research or theory in their discipline. What Andresen describes is the process of inquiry-based learning about teaching.

Based on a study exploring the conceptions academic staff hold about the scholarship of teaching, Trigwell, Martin, Benjamin, and Prosser (2000) found that these conceptions vary according to the extent to which staff hold a teacher-focused versus student-focused conception of teaching, draw on relevant research or theory to inform their knowledge, focus their reflection on specific or more generic issues, and disseminate their findings. There

NEW DIRECTIONS FOR TEACHING AND LEARNING, no. 107, Fall 2006 © Wiley Periodicals, Inc.
Published online in Wiley InterScience (www.interscience.wiley.com) • DOI: 10.1002/tl.246

are obvious similarities in how participants in the Trigwell and associates' study and Andresen understand the notion of scholarship in teaching.

The increasingly popular notion of evidence-based (or informed) practice also helps to further illuminate the meaning of inquiry-based learning about teaching as espoused in this chapter. In line with the most widespread meaning of this notion, evidence-based practice describes a form of teaching that is guided by what has been shown to work well. The "evidence" may lie in formal or informal (less systematically gathered) "data" that were collected, or in an already existing theoretical explanation or interpretation that was developed about a given phenomenon. Often the scholarship of teaching and learning is understood as teachers seeking evidence for what works and then making their findings more widely available through various forms of dissemination so that others can use and build upon them (Huber and Hutchings, 2005). A slightly different interpretation of evidence-based practice focuses explicitly on the notion of reflection in and about learning and teaching. The main concern, according to this latter interpretation of evidence-based practice, lies in the internal cognitive processes that underpin a person's teaching practice. Of particular importance is the question of whether the forms of reflection teachers engage in are suitable for validating knowledge claims (Kreber, 2005). Hence, this perspective suggests that it is essential that teachers seek evidence for the assumptions that guide their practice. In addition, as has been argued elsewhere, in order to assess whether or not teachers engage in evidence-based teaching, and to support them in and reward them for these efforts, we need to focus on whether their engagement in teaching shows evidence of such reflective processes (Kreber, 2006).

This perspective distinguishes three types or levels of reflection, which have been referred to as content, process, and premise reflection (see also Cranton, 1994; Mezirow, 1991). Only the latter two are geared at testing validity claims underlying our knowledge of learning and teaching. The first level of reflection, content reflection, helps us to identify or articulate what we already assume to be true. For example, if I ask myself "What do I know about student motivation?" and in response state that "Students learn much better if exam pressures are high," I make my assumption explicit and as such, surely have engaged in "reflection"; however, this form of reflection has not helped me to further my own, let alone anyone else's, knowledge, as it has led essentially to nothing more than me making an assertion. Teaching portfolios, which have become much more widespread in recent years, at times can be criticized for not demonstrating staff's reflection beyond this first level. Nevertheless, it should be stressed that content reflection is far from insignificant, for often we may not even be aware of the assumptions that guide our practice (Mezirow, 1991).

Process reflection, on the other hand, questions the effectiveness of our approaches or problem-solving strategy, and premise reflection questions the underlying presupposition informing our practice. It is premise reflection that underlies Andresen's notion of critical reflectivity. The above example of "student motivation to learn being greatly enhanced when exam pressure is high" might be useful again here as a tool to illustrate the meaning of each process and premise reflection. The crucial distinction is that process reflection takes the premise (or presupposition) articulated through content reflection for granted, whereas premise reflection, as the term itself suggests, calls this premise into question. The example that follows is meant (only) to illustrate this crucial difference between content, process, and premise reflection.

Given that a teacher holds the assumption that "student motivation to learn is greatly enhanced when exam pressure is high," this teacher, when engaged in process reflection, may ask "How effective am I in simulating a similar context of alertness to assessment throughout the semester so that students do feel motivated to learn or prepare for class?" (Although this question will strike some readers as absurd, note that the question itself is based on the core premise articulated in content reflection.) In contrast, a person involved in premise reflection may ask, "Why do I think that alertness to formal assessment is the best motivator for student learning. What might be alternative ways of motivating students to engage with the material?" To be clear, asking process reflection questions can lead to important learning. An economics teacher who asks herself, "How effective am I in helping students understand the reasons for the unequal distribution of wealth around the world?" or an English teacher who asks himself, "How effective or conscientious have I been in choosing appropriate learning goals for my comparative literature course?" or an engineering teacher who asks, "How effective is my use of computer simulations in order to demonstrate the rules of static?" and seeks information on this question in a variety of ways engages in process reflection. Consequently, process reflection and premise reflection questions allow us to test the validity of our assumptions (Kreber, 2006). However, as was shown, it is only through premise reflection, or critical reflection, that we scrutinize our core assumption or presupposition. The process of questioning and testing the validity of our knowledge claims through process or premise reflection leads to either a verification or contradiction of our assumptions, the latter offering an opportunity for further growth.

## Reflective Practice as Evidence-Based

Much educational literature links the notion of reflection to professional and practical experience (Schön, 1983). However, it has been argued that in order to develop a richer and more fully informed perspective on their practice, teachers need to have access not only to their personal, intuitive, or experience-based knowledge about teaching and learning in their field but also to formal or theory-based knowledge about teaching and learning (Kreber, 2002). When academics engage in reflection on university pedagogy, they would draw not only on their personal (and collective) experiences of teaching the subject but also, to the extent that they are aware of it, on educational research findings and literature, much of which will be discipline-specific and some more generic. Reflection in the process of inquiry-based learning about teaching, therefore, may really be just as much directed at, and informed by, formal knowledge of teaching and learning as it is directed at, and informed by, personal experience. Most academics have a wealth of experience-based knowledge about teaching to draw on to further their professional development and inform their reflections. Much of it is discipline- or subject-specific, but many faculty have experience teaching beyond their own discipline by contributing to liberal arts programs or service-learning courses (see also Huber in Chapter Seven of this volume), or simply by team-teaching interdisciplinary courses; these activities provide them with more general experience-based knowledge about teaching. Nevertheless, rather few have received a thorough preparation for teaching that would have laid a firm foundation with respect to formal discipline-specific and generic knowledge about pedagogy. However, it is only the combination of the two that would fulfill Andresen's second criterion of a scholarship of teaching, namely, that such scholarship would require a deep knowledge base.

In summary, when teachers engage in inquiry-based learning about teaching through content, process, and premise reflection, they may draw on, first, their experience-based knowledge of teaching, and second, formal or theory-based knowledge of pedagogy to provide evidence for the validity of their assumptions. The nature of their knowledge about teaching is partly discipline-specific (for example, students' misconceptions of physics problems) and partly generic (for example, Perry's stages of intellectual development).

## Necessary Domains of Knowledge

What domains of knowledge do teachers need to provide meaningful learning environments for students? Next to content knowledge of the discipline and the ability to construct and advance such knowledge, the knowledge base of teaching, then, also includes discipline-specific and generic pedagogical knowledge. Yet what do we mean by the latter? I suggest it consists of three parts.

The first aspect of discipline-specific and generic knowledge about pedagogy relates to knowledge of teaching and assessment methods. Increased class size and greater diversity of students make the process of assessment and teaching much more complex and difficult than in the past. Disciplines that rely largely on discursive pedagogies and written essays as the main forms of assessment are particularly challenged by the effects of mass higher education, but assessment is not necessarily any less demanding in physics labs, where incoming students may not have received the necessary background preparation for recording and interpreting data. Most generally, as classes are getting too big and knowledge continues to grow exponentially, available teaching time appears to be getting increasingly shorter, and many teachers perceive little opportunity to deviate much from a pure transmission approach to their teaching. Yet if the goal is to bring teaching and research closer together (based on the assumption that such a link would enhance both research and teaching), the transmission approach (teacher-focused and oriented toward content knowledge) may not be the most effective approach. Clearly, teachers will benefit from identifying and questioning prevailing pedagogies by learning about and developing possible alternatives. Discussing how to employ inquiry-based learning (see Part Two of this volume) in large classes would seem particularly important.

The second aspect of discipline-specific and generic knowledge about pedagogy relates to knowledge of how students learn. Over the past decade there has been a strong interest in learning (Barr and Tagg, 1995), and this domain of pedagogical knowledge is now recognized as important as is knowledge of teaching and assessment methods. Given today's diverse student population, it is important that teachers develop knowledge not only of how traditional undergraduate students learn and can be assisted in their learning, but also, increasingly, of how to support the learning of nontraditional students. A key issue with respect to fostering student motivation, for example, would be to understand how to help all students to perceive the subject as relevant to their respective aspirations and needs. It is likewise important to understand the challenges different students experience in researching a subject. What do they struggle with when engaged in inquiry-based learning in this field, and why?

Finally, the third aspect of discipline-specific and generic knowledge about pedagogy relates to knowledge of the goals and purposes of the courses we teach and of higher education more generally. In an era when conflicting external demands pull higher education institutions in multiple directions, this third domain of teaching knowledge, which essentially addresses the philosophical aspects of teaching, is clearly no less critical to the knowledge base of teaching as is knowledge of student learning or knowledge of teaching and assessment methods. When Andresen (2000) argues that the scholarship of teaching requires opening any claims regarding knowledge about the "why" of teaching to proper intellectual challenge, he is thinking of this third knowledge domain. When we explore why research and teaching links should be strengthened in undergraduate programs, we are directly involved in reflecting on the goals and purposes of university education.

## Why Engage in Inquiry-Based Learning About Teaching

There are six arguments in favor of the proposition that those who teach in higher education institutions should engage in inquiry-based learning about teaching. First, inquiry-based learning about teaching in one's subject area can be as intellectually stimulating and internally rewarding as traditional research in the discipline. Second, creating meaningful and effective learning experiences for all students needs to be recognized as a professional obligation of those who teach. Third, there is some evidence that there exist more external rewards for inquiry-based learning about teaching today than in the past (and greater opportunities to learn about and share this work). Fourth, inquiry-based learning about teaching provides solutions to context-specific problems, something seminars, workshops, books, or articles are less likely to provide. Fifth, if facilitated well, inquiry-based learning about teaching can bring the department more closely together in the pursuit of common purposes. Finally, as Huber argues in Chapter Seven of this volume, inquiry-based learning about teaching in the disciplines may also benefit the disciplines themselves in that it carries the potential to call into question knowledge practices that are taken for granted and to identify new ones.

## The Role of Educational Development Units

Most fundamentally, educational developers will need to be perceived as having the expertise necessary to support such work (see also Castley in Chapter Three of this volume). This perception involves that they are seen as experienced teachers, knowledgeable in educational theory and research methodology suitable for exploring issues of learning and teaching. Particularly at research-intensive institutions, their credibility will be judged also by the extent to which they have contributed to the advancement of knowledge within their own field of study. Next to such expertise, educational developers also need well-developed interpersonal skills and knowledge of how to work with colleagues who, despite being experts (often of international repute) in their own disciplines, are learning about a field they are not yet familiar with and one they therefore perceive as posing multiple challenges as well as risks of appearing foolish, ignorant, or even worse, incompetent in the eyes of teaching and learning "experts" by whom they feel judged. Some knowledge of adult learners' unique needs may therefore be an advantage. An atmosphere of collegiality and collaboration, rather than a "judge-mentality" that so often characterizes the teacher-student relationship in higher education, ought to guide educational development initiatives aimed at involving staff in inquiry-based learning about their teaching.

## Specific Educational Program Initiatives

There are several ways in which educational development units (EDUs) can support teachers' engagement in inquiry-based learning about pedagogy. First, they can offer professional programs for both inexperienced and experienced staff (including sessionals and graduate students) at the certificate, diploma, or master's level that introduce them to formal knowledge teaching and assessment methods, learning and student development, and different curriculum perspectives (the latter focusing on the various purposes and goals of higher education in today's complex world). Course activities and assignments could be designed such that they directly involve participants in content, process, and premise reflection on issues they are confronted with in their own practice and that draw on both their experiential knowledge and the theories or recent research introduced to inform these reflections (see Kreber, 2001). For example, staff could be asked to experiment with an innovative pedagogy (such as problem-based learning), collect data on its effectiveness, and explain the results on the basis of both their (recently acquired) formal knowledge and their experience-based knowledge about pedagogy. Introducing staff to various classroom assessment techniques (Angelo and Cross, 1993) and ways of carrying out classroom research (Cross and Steadman, 1996) would constitute particularly important aspects of the course or program. In recent years we have come to acknowledge the importance of the disciplines in furthering our understanding of learning and teaching (Donald, 2002; Jenkins, 1996; Pace and Middendorf, 2004). It follows that such courses should also include opportunities for participants to explore the nature of learning in their respective subject areas. Although course activities could include groups of staff from the same discipline discussing relevant issues, working on assignments, and later sharing their insights across disciplinary groups, their experience-based personal and collective knowledge about teaching and learning should be complemented and enriched by the ever-growing discipline-specific pedagogical literature in their field. Natural questions to address would include the following: How is learning in a physics course different from learning in an English literature course? How do different subject areas understand the nature of a concept? What makes a concept difficult to understand? What are the basic learning tasks in different disciplines? What methods are suitable to best facilitate learning? And what might be good ways of exploring whether or not one has been effective with helping students learn?

At the master's level, a course in educational research methodology introducing participants to different genres of research (see also D'Andrea in Chapter Nine of this volume for a more thorough discussion of methodological issues) and a supervised thesis would be the natural way of supporting staff in the conduct of more rigorous research on learning and teaching. Again, discipline-specific pedagogical journal articles or books would be an important learning resource. The unique ways in which the research traditions of the various disciplines can inform inquiry about teaching should be brought to the fore as much as possible (Huber and Morreale, 2002).

Second, informal monthly reading circles where an interesting article or book chapter is discussed, if skillfully facilitated, can provide plenty of opportunity to foster content, process, and premise reflection among participants. Particularly if the reading circle is open to teachers (including faculty, sessionals, and graduate students) from all departments on campus, their varied perspectives on the issues raised in the text can be strong triggers of reflection.

Third, providing actual examples of inquiry-based learning about teaching is important. Examples should illustrate the wide range of possible approaches from different disciplines. Staff should be encouraged to explore what questions different disciplines raise and whether they could learn from each other (see also Chapter Seven in this volume). Bringing in speakers from other campuses that have similar programs in place, preferably who are also faculty members who can talk about their experiences of engaging in inquiry-based learning about teaching, would seem particularly worthwhile. Developing videos that show what this kind of work looks like in practice and how it unfolds (from the design phase right through the action, interpretation, and re-implementation phase) would be meaningful. Publishing a high-quality newsletter or journal in which staff can disseminate the results of such work more widely among colleagues within and across their department could be very motivating to others to follow their example.

Fourth, making competitive grants available for the development of pedagogical innovations and discipline-specific pedagogical research, particularly to those who have participated in the professional development programs described earlier, could be a strong incentive for further engagement in such work. Though there is nothing inherently wrong with supporting individual enthusiasts, it is often desirable to support teams of colleagues in inquiry-based learning projects, as the results are more likely to become firmly integrated into departmental practice.

Fifth, directly linked to the previous point is the need for EDUs to gain the support of heads of departments and senior administrators (for example, the academic vice president, pro-vice-chancellor, or university president). The latter need to be convinced that pedagogical innovations and quality enhancement in teaching are likely to occur if adequate levels of funding are made available for inquiries by staff that help them to better understand how students learn and how to support their learning. (In this climate of intensified performance accountability, senior administrators may look favorably on schemes that would also demonstrate to external assessors that the institution explicitly supports such enhancement of teaching quality.) The former need to recognize that providing funds without also providing the time needed to engage in such important development opportunities is clearly not sufficient to enhance teaching and learning. Allocating necessary time would involve not penalizing staff for not publishing in their discipline while engaged in inquiry-based learning projects about teaching (though such efforts may eventually lead to dissemination of results in more pedagogically or practically oriented venues). Furthermore, heads of department would need to be convinced that inquiry-based learning about teaching is serious scholarly work and should be rewarded as such.

Sixth, rather than administering awards for teaching excellence based on past performance of either individual staff members or groups of staff, it might be more desirable for EDUs to focus their efforts on launching a teaching fellowship scheme where the award is directly tied to a proposed inquiry project that is perceived to spark pedagogical innovations in the department. Although the advantages of offering more opportunities for discipline-specific educational development are widely recognized, such support can often be provided only on a case-by-case basis as educational development staff, evidently, cannot cover all the content expertise represented in the various departments on campus. However, this resource and expertise problem could be greatly reduced by conferring to teaching fellows the status of faculty associates to the EDU, at least for the time that they are involved in their inquiry-based project. These associates would then constitute an important liaison between the EDU and the departments.

Seventh, EDUs would play a significant role in organizing institutional conferences that allow staff from different disciplines to share and demonstrate what they have learned from their inquiry-based projects. This initiative would also prepare staff for participating in national and international conferences on university pedagogy (Lund University in Sweden, for example, has followed this model for several years). Surely, the EDU could encourage departments to organize their own events and to publicize the inquiry-based learning about teaching projects their staff are engaged in through departmental bulletin boards, Web sites, and discussion groups, and the faculty associate again would play an important role in this regard.

## Concluding Comment

As the chapters in Part Two of this volume argue persuasively, one promising way to prepare students adequately for their personal, professional, and civic roles in later life is to engage them directly in the process of problem-based or inquiry-based learning. In order to engage them effectively, faculty (but also others with teaching responsibilities, such as graduate students, postdocs, and sessional instructors) require meaningful opportunities to learn about how to best facilitate this process. Inquiry-based learning about teaching (or the scholarship of teaching and learning) will eventually help faculty better understand how to support students effectively in their learning. Reflection, and specifically premise or critical reflection (see also Elton in Chapter Four of this volume), on our present knowledge and practices in relation to the goals and purposes of teaching, pedagogies and assessment methods, and student learning, plays an important role in the process. Interactions not only with colleagues but also with the rapidly expanding literature on teaching and learning, both discipline-specific and more generic, inform and support inquiry-based learning about teaching in significant ways.

## References

Andresen, L. W. "A Usable, Trans-Disciplinary Conception of Scholarship." *Higher Education Research and Development,* 2000, *19*(2), 137–153.

Angelo, T., and Cross, P. *Classroom Assessment Techniques: A Handbook for College Teachers.* (2nd ed.) San Francisco: Jossey-Bass, 1993.

Barr, R. B., and Tagg, J. "From Teaching to Learning: A New Paradigm for Undergraduate Education." *Change,* 1995, *27,* 13–25.

Cranton, P. A. *Understanding and Promoting Transformative Learning: A Guide for Educators of Adults.* San Francisco: Jossey-Bass, 1994.

Cross, P., and Steadman, M. *Classroom Research: Implementing the Scholarship of Teaching.* San Francisco: Jossey-Bass, 1996.

Donald, J. G. *Learning to Think: Disciplinary Perspectives.* San Francisco: Jossey-Bass, 2002.

Huber, M., and Hutchings, P. *The Advancements of Learning: Building the Teaching Commons: The Carnegie Report on the Scholarship of Teaching and Learning.* San Francisco: Jossey-Bass, 2005.

Huber, M. T., and Morreale, S. P. (eds.). *Disciplinary Styles in the Scholarship of Teaching and Learning: Exploring Common Ground.* Washington, D.C.: American Association for Higher Education, 2002.

Jenkins, A. "Discipline-Based Educational Development." *International Journal of Academic Development,* 1996, *1*(1), 50–62.

Kreber, C. "Building the Scholarship of Teaching into Faculty Development and Graduate Education." In C. Kreber (ed.), *Scholarship Revisited: Perspectives on the Scholarship of Teaching."* New Directions for Teaching and Learning, no. 86. San Francisco: Jossey-Bass, 2001.

Kreber, C. "Teaching Excellence, Teaching Expertise, and the Scholarship of Teaching." *Innovative Higher Education,* 2002, *27*(1), 5–23.

Kreber, C. "Reflection on Teaching and the Scholarship of Teaching." *Higher Education,* 2005, *50*(2), 323–359.

Kreber, C. "Developing the Scholarship of Teaching Through Transformative Learning." *Journal of the Scholarship of Teaching and Learning,* 2006, *6*(1).

Mezirow. J. *Transformative Dimensions of Adult Learning.* San Francisco: Jossey-Bass, 1991.

Pace, D., and Middendorf, J. (eds.). *Decoding the Disciplines: Helping Students Learn Disciplinary Ways of Thinking.* New Directions for Teaching and Learning, no. 28. San Francisco: Jossey-Bass, 2004.

Schön, D. *The Reflective Practitioner: How Professionals Think in Action.* San Francisco: Jossey-Bass, 1983.

Trigwell, K., Martin, E., Benjamin, J., and Prosser, M. "Scholarship of Teaching: A Model." *Higher Education Research and Development,* 2000, *19*(2), 155–168.

*CAROLIN KREBER is director of the Centre for Teaching, Learning and Assessment at the University of Edinburgh, where she is also professor of teaching and learning in higher education in the Department of Higher and Community Education.*

9

*Pedagogical inquiry on teaching and learning in higher education is best served by methodological approaches that produce purposeful questions and engage in systematic analysis.*

# Exploring Methodological Issues Related to Pedagogical Inquiry in Higher Education

*Vaneeta-marie D'Andrea*

> There is undoubtedly some pretty bad educational research; quite a lot of it is published and some of it has been taken up as established knowledge.
>
> H. Goldstein (1998, p. 33)

How many times have you seen or heard the view that educational research in the United Kingdom is really not up to standard or value for money? A recent paper by Gorard (2001) includes a summary of similar observations by a wide range of researchers. Illustrative of these views is the conclusion that there has not been a systematic "development of a comprehensive body of high-quality evidence" (Millett, 1997; see also Sotto, 1998). Another study cited by Gorard (2001) claims that one factor contributing to this situation is the limited educational research capacity in the United Kingdom due to the "lack of developed research expertise among the people involved" (McIntyre and McIntyre, 2000).

Although much of this discussion on the quality of educational research concerns research on primary and secondary education, similar examples are available in the higher education sector as well. For example, in my role as a peer reviewer for a number of higher education journals, I find that more and more I am asked to review papers that often have barely

NEW DIRECTIONS FOR TEACHING AND LEARNING, no. 107, Fall 2006 © Wiley Periodicals, Inc.
Published online in Wiley InterScience (www.interscience.wiley.com) • DOI: 10.1002/tl.247

89

a hint of the question being investigated and no rationale for the methodological approach taken to investigate the question; as for methods of inquiry, it often appears that the author assumes that a bit of interviewing in combination with some sort of questionnaire is expected of any study of teaching and learning. When empirical data are collected in this haphazard way, how could anyone expect them to have explanatory power? How useful are a study's "findings" in this context? Yet how many times do we read papers that attempt to make claims on the basis of flimsy evidence? You will notice I am avoiding using the notion "to generalize"; this is a longer story for another time.

But before I am pilloried for these observations, let me confirm that I do not mean to suggest that there is only one appropriate methodological approach to conducting educational research. I have found myself misunderstood on this point many times and derisively labelled an "unrepentant positivist" (it is interesting to see how this has come to be a term of derision in the seemingly open-minded academic world; see also Gorard, 2001). In fact, if I can be labeled anything, I would most likely be called an unrepentant grounded theorist, and, yes, I have also been chided for this as well. Nevertheless, I will try not to bias this piece with my methodological preferences; rather, I wish to pick up from where Kreber left off in Chapter Eight and focus on the choices that need to be made in order to conduct pedagogical investigations that can add value to this body of knowledge.

As I see it, there are two major lessons to be learned from a review of the state of generic educational research that apply to this discussion. These were articulated in the first paragraph of this chapter: first, higher education pedagogic investigators need to find a way to develop a comprehensive body of high-quality evidence, and second, we need to ensure that these investigators are given the necessary research expertise to produce high-quality studies. Each of these issues is, in turn, the focus of the last two sections of the chapter.

First, however, this chapter starts by looking at a few of the key debates surrounding investigations into teaching and learning in higher education, and it raises a series of questions related to engaging in pedagogical inquiry. It draws most of its references from the United Kingdom, with a few from North America as well. It ends with some suggestions to support the development of a rigorous scholarship of teaching and learning.

## Key Debates Surrounding Investigations into Teaching and Learning in Higher Education

So far we have been speaking in general terms about educational research. I would now like to focus the discussion more specifically on higher education and even more precisely on inquiries into teaching and learning in higher education. Earlier work carried out with other colleagues (Gordon, D'Andrea, Gosling, and Stefani, 2003; D'Andrea and Gosling, 2005) has considered a range of terms and their related definitions that are currently used in the literature on teaching and learning in higher education to refer to

NEW DIRECTIONS FOR TEACHING AND LEARNING • DOI: 10.1002/tl

inquiries into teaching and learning. I emphasize "used in the literature on teaching and learning" since it has been found that faculty and staff are rarely familiar with this specialist jargon employed mostly by educational-ists (see Gordon, D'Andrea, Gosling, and Stefani, 2003; Stierer and Anto-niou, 2004). What is important from my standpoint is not what faculty or staff call the inquiries they carry out or whether or not they are familiar with the educational jargon; these points are far less important than the ways in which their pedagogical investigations are conceptualized and investigated and the fact that they are doing them at all, which I will discuss more later. In order to help set out the parameters of this chapter, I will summarize the major issues explored and the conclusions reported in the pedagogic liter-ature before moving on to a discussion of the structure and process of ped-agogical inquiry in higher education.

## Ped-D, Ped-R, and SoTL

Is it Ped-D, Ped-R, SoTL, or just plain, old-fashioned intellectual curiosity and reflection? This question includes some of the key terms applied to ped-agogical inquiry in higher education in the United Kingdom. Because this area of work is an emerging field, precise definitions of what constitutes ped-agogical inquiry or what it is called remain open to discussion and debate (see Stierer and Antoniou, 2004). For the purposes of this discussion, how-ever, I will begin by drawing on the work of Gordon and colleagues (2003). In their study, they attempt to identify distinguishing characteristics for each of the key terms: pedagogical development (Ped-D), pedagogical research (Ped-R), and the scholarship of teaching and learning (SoTL).

> The first point to make is that PedD and PedR have a common focus or con-tent. This focus/content is the relationship between teaching, learning, and the learner and subject matter, within the context of higher education. . . . Secondly, these terms, 'PedD' and 'PedR,' do not refer to entirely distinct and clearly demarcated areas of practice or discourse. On the contrary, they denote overlapping sets of activities. Both terms can refer to activities, or to the out-puts that derive from these activities. There is a considerable overlap between the activities and the outputs. . . . PedD and PedR represent different character-istics, or different emphases, within what we call 'dimensions of inquiry' [See Table 9.1 below.] The common focus and the overlapping activities and out-puts form the 'broad canopy' of Scholarship of Teaching and Learning. . . . We suggest that the terms may be used to denote different features of inquiry within the broader field of SoTL. (Gordon, D'Andrea, Gosling, and Stefani, 2003, p. 24)

The relationship between these three terms and the larger research and teaching nexus in higher education was further considered in later work by D'Andrea and Gosling (2005). They note, "From our perspective the SoTL overlaps both Ped R and Ped D which in turn are situated in the

### Table 9.1. Dimensions of Pedagogical Development and Pedagogical Research

|  | *Ped D* | *Ped R* |
| --- | --- | --- |
| Activity | Aim to improve practice | Aim to describe, analyze, conceptualize |
|  | Informal methodology | Formal research proposal |
|  | Context specific | Applicable to wider contexts |
|  | Own teaching/own department | Independent of own teaching |
|  | Aimed at local audience | Aimed at national or international audience |
|  | Pragmatic, low theorization | Based on established theory |
|  | Subject-focused or generic | Subject-focused or generic |
| Outputs | Improvement to practice | Better understanding of practice |
|  | Limited generalizability | Generalizable output |
|  | Non-refereed publication | Peer-reviewed publication |
|  | Guidelines on good practice | Analytic description/conceptualization |
|  | For own institution use | Results in the public domain |
|  | Web site | May be reported on Web site |
|  | Publication | Publication |

*Source:* Gordon, D'Andrea, Gosling, and Stefani (2003)

middle circle of a Venn diagram linking research and teaching. We are suggesting that SoTL is the bridge between research and teaching because it encompasses both Ped R and Ped D" (2005, pp. 157–158). This idea is represented in Figure 9.1.

Whatever this activity is called or however it is defined, there are two important points: first, there are increasing numbers of faculty and staff who are interested in investigating the work they do as teachers; second, there is now an agenda in higher education to pursue knowledge of teaching and learning both for the purpose of its development and improvement and for the advancement of scholarship. I refrain from calling this activity research per se because to do so would require a fuller discussion of the categories Boyer (1990) sets up, which the limits of space do not allow; instead, I simply refer to this activity as pedagogic inquiry or the scholarship of teaching and learning. Next I take a look at some of the issues related to the process for taking these scholarly investigations forward.

## Methods and Methodological Approaches and Pedagogical Inquiry

Producing high-quality studies to form the foundation of a comprehensive body of evidence on pedagogic knowledge in higher education requires a basic understanding of methodological approaches and the methods used to engage in these inquiries. Stierer and Antoniou (2004) have stated: "We

## Figure 9.1. Ped-D, Ped-R and SoTL.

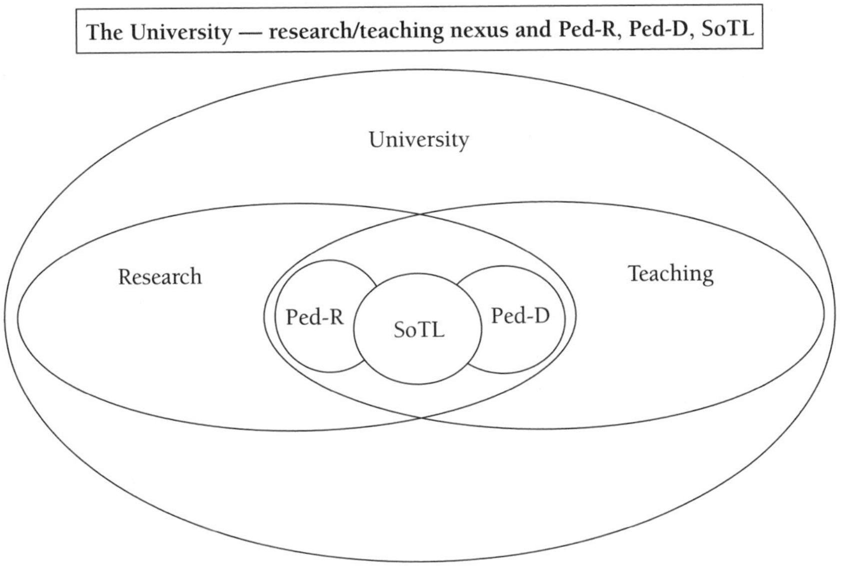

The University — research/teaching nexus and Ped-R, Ped-D, SoTL

*Source:* D'Andrea and Gosling, 2005, p. 158.

speculate that methodologies for pedagogic research in HE may be distinctive (even if the research methods used are not). . . . We conclude that the main defining feature of methodologies for pedagogic research in HE is their diversity and the opportunities they offer to combine conventional educational research methodologies with HE teachers' disciplinary expertise and understandings" (p. 275; see also Chapter Seven in this volume).

This latter point cannot be emphasized enough: involvement with the SoTL, as Huber has pointed out in Chapter Seven of this volume, provides the opportunity for higher education pedagogic investigators to take a lead in educational research, first, by broadening the methodological approaches used and the methods employed through finding ways to use the full array of disciplinary methodological approaches, and second, by using the subject groupings to create a comprehensive body of evidence, as is being started by the United Kingdom's Higher Education Academy's Subject Network.

These developments are particularly opportune in light of the recent findings by Pascarella and Terenzini (1991, 2005), two United States researchers who have twice compiled comprehensive volumes summarizing research on higher education in the United States. In both publications, they have come to a similar conclusion, that "traditional quantitative approaches dominate the research, regardless of topic" (2005, p. 636; see also Biggs, 1993; Candy, 1993; and Gorard, 2001). A more eclectic approach that utilizes the multiplicity of approaches available from all subject fields

NEW DIRECTIONS FOR TEACHING AND LEARNING • DOI: 10.1002/tl

would contribute to making these pedagogical scholarly investigations more likely to meet the needs of these subjects and expand the range of approaches used in the investigations.

Moreover, as Gorard (2001) states, "It is particularly important for the well-being of educational research that we do not waste time in methodological paradigm wars. . . . In particular we need to overcome the false dualism of 'quantitative' and 'qualitative' approaches. . . . Words can be counted and numbers can be descriptive" (p. 31; see also Coser, 1975). Therefore, this chapter does not consider the tired debate surrounding this dichotomous definition of research methodologies; rather, it attempts to illustrate the importance of what I view is the most basic issue related to doing quality studies on teaching and learning in higher education: framing the research question itself (see Taylor, 1993). No matter what disciplinary methodologies are selected, in all cases it is essential to be able to start by clearly identifying the following elements: the teaching and learning question to be investigated, how it was conceptualized within the context of the subject being taught, the rationale for its consideration and its potential for improving teaching and learning, the scholarly work on this aspect of teaching and learning that has preceded it (Sotto, 1998), and the reason it is an important question to explore.

Concentrating time and effort on conceptualizing the pedagogical question is the first step in determining the investigative design. From the articles I have reviewed, it appears to me that this simple first step is often ignored, overlooked, or rushed in an effort to get on with the investigation. This procedure of carefully considering the question (or questions), rather than delaying the investigation, can help to move the process along, because through clarifying the question the methodological approach to answer it becomes easier to identify. Selecting a particular approach and appropriate methods to go with it can sometimes be a bit overwhelming, considering the array of useful approaches and methods available to scholars of teaching and learning and outlined in the standard texts in the field (Gordon, 1996; Scott and Usher, 1999; Cohen, Manion, and Morrison, 2000).

As Wilson (2001) has pointed out, "There is no single model of inquiry into education, no single method of procedure on which the researcher can rely in any and every case" (p. 333). If pedagogic scholars are encouraged to use the tools of their trade (subject-related methodologies and methods) this challenge of choice is made much more feasible because the choice is limited not only to something familiar but to something for which the investigator already has specialist skills. What is important to keep foremost in mind while progressing scholarly inquiry into carefully considered questions on teaching and learning is "that our search for answers retains the systematic rigor that only careful scholarship can bring to the understanding" (Bolster, 1983, p. 24).

This section has mainly concerned the basic framing of investigations and briefly outlined one of the key issues related to designing studies. The limits of this chapter do not allow for further consideration of other elements of scholarly investigations; however, before moving on it is important at least to acknowledge the role of theory in the process. As Sotto (1998) has noted, investigations into teaching and learning "should always be considered within the context of a systematic and coherent theory of learning and teaching" (p. 27). Moreover, according to Pascarella and Terenzini (2005), "Theory-free studies offer little in the way of systematic understanding" (p. 631). To paraphrase Coser (1975), if concepts and theoretical notions are weak, no methodology, however precise, will advance our knowledge of teaching and learning in higher education.

## Building a Critical Mass of Expertise in Pedagogic Inquiry in Higher Education

The second lesson learned from the generic education literature centers around the expertise required to carry out pedagogical inquiry. As Goldstein (1998) has noted, "What we need is a greater degree of professionalism among those doing and also funding research (in education). This means that there should be adequate training in research methods involving a partnership with researchers. . . . There has to be recognition that educational research is difficult, time consuming, and requires professional expertise" (p. 34).

Addressing issues of professionalism will vary depending on the faculty or staff in question. If they are highly trained in the research methodologies and methods of their substantive field, then it would seem that encouraging the use of these methodologies and methods, where appropriate, in the pedagogical arena would be one way forward and consistent with developments in the SoTL. Promoting this link between subject and pedagogic approaches of inquiry could easily be integrated into the various activities of EDCs suggested by Kreber in Chapter Seven of this volume (see also D'Andrea and Gosling, 2005). EDC activities also bring faculty and staff together from across disciplinary groupings, creating additional opportunity for the cross-fertilization among the various disciplinary methodologies for investigations of teaching and learning (see Huber, Chapter Seven, and Kreber, Chapter Eight in this volume).

Rice (1992) has stated, "All faculty ought to be scholars in this broader sense, deepening their preferred approaches to knowing but constantly pressing, and being pressed by peers, to enlarge their scholarly capacities and encompass other—often contrary ways—of knowing" (p. 126).

In other words, one important way to professionalize the scholarly inquiry of higher education is to engage with those methodologies we know best from our subject disciplines and to learn from our colleagues about theirs. Kreber (2000) has noted that "Acquiring scholarship in teaching is a learning process involving various combinations of instrumental, but primarily, communicative and emancipatory learning processes. . . . Professors validate their knowledge about teaching through critical discourse within a community of peers. One could perhaps conclude that learning about one's discipline and learning about teaching are two processes that inform each other and are inextricably intertwined" (p. 75).

In addition to institutional-level efforts to professionalize pedagogical inquiry, in the United Kingdom there is a major, national-level initiative in the social sciences sponsored by the Teaching and Learning Research Program (TLRP) of the Economic and Social Research Council (ESRC). As described by Gorard (2001), the Research Capacity-Building (RCB) project "is an innovative attempt to invigorate an entire research field. Among its aims are to support and encourage: the management of complex projects, a widening of methodological approaches, the further combination of different approaches from different contributory disciplines, the melding of theory-building and method, and the creation of new models for transforming findings into usable forms. These aims are not unique to educational research, much less teaching and learning research" (p. 2).

One of several goals of the program is to engage in the articulation and combination of qualitative approaches with quantitative studies. It is the view of the program, according to Gorard (2002a), that "What is needed is more researchers able and motivated to use, read, and critique work based on all methods. This probably involves an increase in the number *and* quality of researchers with quantitative skills, and an increase in the quality of researchers with qualitative skills" (p. 4).

The full range of RCB activities to support the development of this increased capacity for informed inquiry into teaching and learning in the sector includes regional meetings, publications, skills consultations, skills training, and workshops. This list is impressive on its own; given enough time, it should contribute significantly to the professionalization of pedagogic inquiry.

Another ESRC initiative is aimed at increasing professional expertise at the individual level and at the very start of an academic career during PhD training. All ESRC-funded PhDs are now required to have at least initial master's level research training, which includes learning how to "use, model, and interpret multivariate statistical data" (Gorard, 2002b, p. 2). However, Deem and Lucas (2006) report that this development "is not universally supported or favoured. . . . Much research on teaching research methods focuses on doctoral research students and pays little attention to the learning of methods itself" (p. 4).

Nevertheless, all in all, current efforts at the individual, institutional, and national levels in the United Kingdom to increase the capacity of expertise in pedagogic inquiry bodes well for this endeavor and for those of us committed to improving student learning in higher education through the scholarship of teaching and learning. As Boyer (1987) has stated, "Scholarship is not an esoteric appendage; it is the heart of what the profession is all about. All faculty, throughout their careers, should themselves remain students. As scholars they must continue to learn and be seriously and continuously engaged in the expanding intellectual world" (p. 131).

# References

Biggs, J. B. "From Theory to Practice: A Cognitive Systems Approach." *Higher Education Research and Development,* 1993, *12*(1), 73–85.

Bolster, A. S., Jr. "Toward a More Effective Model of Research on Teaching." *Harvard Educational Review,* 1983, *53*(3), 294–308.

Boyer, E. L. *College: The Undergraduate Experience in America.* New York: HarperCollins, 1987.

Boyer, E. *Scholarship Reconsidered.* Stanford, Calif.: Carnegie Foundation for the Advancement of Teaching, 1990.

Candy, P. "Learning Theories in Higher Education: Reflections on the Keynote Day, HERDSA 1992." *Higher Education Research and Development,* 1993, *12*(1), 99–106.

Cohen, L., Manion, L., and Morrison, K. *Research Methods in Education.* (5th ed.) London: Routledge Falmer, 2000.

Coser, L. "Two Methods in Search of Substance." Presidential address delivered at the Annual Meeting of the American Sociological Association, San Francisco, Aug. 1975.

D'Andrea, V-m., and Gosling, D. *Improving Teaching and Learning in Higher Education: A Whole Institution Approach.* Maidenhead, United Kingdom: Society for Research into Higher Education and Open University Press, 2005.

Deem, R., and Lucas, L. "Learning About Research: Exploring the Learning and Teaching/Research Relationship Amongst Educational Practitioners Studying in Higher Education." *Teaching in Higher Education,* 2006, *11*(1), 1–18.

Goldstein, H. "'Yes, But . . .' The Importance of Educational Research." *Improving Schools,* 1998, *1*(2), 33–34.

Gorard, S. "A Changing Climate for Educational Research? The Role of Research Capacity Building." Occasional Paper Series, paper 45. Cardiff: Cardiff University School of Social Science, 2001.

Gorard, S. "How Do We Overcome the Methodological Schism (or Can There Be a 'Compleat' Researcher)?" Occasional Paper Series, paper 47. Cardiff: Cardiff University School of Social Science, 2002a.

Gorard, S. "Introduction to the ESRC TLRP Research Capacity-Building Network." *Building Research Capacity,* 2002b, *1*(1), 2–3.

Gordon, G., D'Andrea, V-m., Gosling, D., and Stefani, L. *Building Capacity for Change in Higher Education: Research on the Scholarship of Teaching.* Bristol: Higher Education Funding Council for England, 2003.

Gordon, P. (ed.). *A Guide to Educational Research.* London: Woburn Press, 1996.

Kreber, C. "How Teaching Award Winners Conceptualize Academic Work: Further Thoughts on the Meaning of Scholarship." *Teaching in Higher Education,* 2000, *5*(1), 61–78.

McIntryre, D., and McIntryre, A. "Capacity for Research into Teaching and Learning." Report to TLRP, 2000.

Millett, A. Speech to TTA Research Conference, London, Dec. 5, 1997.

Pascarella, E. T., and Terenzini, P. T. *How College Affects Students: Findings and Insights from Twenty Years of Research.* San Francisco: Jossey-Bass, 1991.

Pascarella, E. T., and Terenzini, P. T. *How College Affects Students: A Third Decade of Research, Volume 2.* San Francisco: Jossey-Bass, 2005.

Rice, G. "Toward a Broader Conception of Scholarship: The American Context." In T. G. Whiston and R. L. Geiger (eds.), *Research and Higher Education: The United States and the United Kingdom.* Maidenhead, United Kingdom: Society for Research into Higher Education and Open University Press, 1992.

Scott, D., and Usher, R. *Researching Education Data, Methods and Theory in Educational Enquiry.* London: Cassell, 1999.

Sotto, E. "On Writing About Teaching in Higher Education." *Psychology Teaching Review,* 1998, *7*(1) 24–31.

Stierer, B., and Antoniou, M. "Are There Distinctive Methodologies for Pedagogic Research in Higher Education?" *Teaching in Higher Education,* 2004, *9*(3) 275–285.

Taylor, G. "A Theory of Practice: Hermeneutical Understanding." *Higher Education Research and Development,* 1993, *12*(1), 59–72.

Wilson, J. "'Data' and 'Theory': Some Conceptual Points." *Educational Research,* 2001, *43*(3), 329–333.

*VANEETA-MARIE D'ANDREA is director of academic affairs and operations and professor of higher education at Central Saint Martins College of Art and Design, London.*

NEW DIRECTIONS FOR TEACHING AND LEARNING • DOI: 10.1002/tl

## 10

*This chapter considers whether there are grounds for believing that an inquiry-based approach to teaching and educational development will enhance practice.*

# The Value of Pedagogic Inquiry for Improving Teaching

*David Gosling*

When faculty are encouraged to engage in pedagogic inquiry, it is normally because it is assumed that both teaching and student learning will be improved as a consequence. In this chapter, we examine this assumption and ask what is implied by it and whether it can be justified. Our discussion examines the relationship between investigation and improved practice and the evidence that practice has been improved by faculty undertaking pedagogic inquiry.

The case for saying that teacher-led pedagogic inquiry is fundamentally about improving practice has been made by Hutchings and Shulman (2000). They argue that when "faculty frame, and systematically investigate questions relating to student learning—the conditions under which it occurs, what it looks like, how it deepens, and so forth," they do so "with an eye not only on improving their classroom but to advancing practice beyond it" (p. 48). According to this view, faculty are motivated to undertake investigation not only by the desire to bring about improvements within the restricted environment of their own teaching but also to contribute to a wider debate about improving teaching.

Theall and Centra (2001) see this improvement occurring through the accumulation of pedagogic knowledge that can be exploited by teachers: "Improvement comes about through the teacher's investigation of specific teaching and learning contexts and this process adds to pedagogical content knowledge by incorporating important factors in teaching and learning across disciplines" (p. 34).

NEW DIRECTIONS FOR TEACHING AND LEARNING, no. 107, Fall 2006  © Wiley Periodicals, Inc.
Published online in Wiley InterScience (www.interscience.wiley.com) • DOI: 10.1002/tl.248

But according to Trigwell and Shale (2004), there is a question whether "expanded pedagogic content knowledge" (or "knowledge about learning") is a necessary and sufficient basis for improving teaching. Rather, they suggest, what is important is "not only a matter of qualitatively increasing what is known about teaching but also a matter of qualitatively enhancing the process of reasoning during teaching" (p. 527). For these authors it is not knowledge about teaching (or learning) that is important, but rather knowledge in teaching, that is, "knowledge how," or action knowledge.

There has been much written about the relationship between different types of knowledge and professional practice (Schön, 1983; Eraut, 1994). Whatever that relationship may turn out to be, there are clear expectations that teachers who systematically undertake investigation into their practice will become better teachers. Such expectations have been made very explicit in the K–12 sector, where practitioner-led research has been called the new professionalism (Hargreaves, 1996; Hillage, Pearson, Erson, and Tamkin, 1998). In the higher education context, Schön (2000) argued, institutions need to legitimize "practitioner's generation of actionable knowledge in the form of models or prototypes that can be carried over, by reflective transfer, to new practice situations (p. 34). Thus, the ultimate justification of an inquiry-led scholarship of teaching is that it produces "expert teachers" who can create "the most powerful student learning" (Trigwell and Shale, 2004, p. 527).

Before we discuss how improved practice can follow from pedagogic inquiry, it is necessary to point out some reasons that we need to be cautious about understanding this relationship. Consider the following model of action learning (adapted from McNiff, 1993):

1. Identify a teaching problem.
2. Imagine a solution to the problem.
3. Implement the solution.
4. Evaluate the solution.
5. Modify ideas and practice in light of the evaluation.

Of course, this model does not suggest that the so-called solution will necessarily be found the first time. It may take several iterations of the action-research circle—observe, plan, act, test—cycle before the improvement occurs (Zuber-Skerritt, 1992). Nevertheless, there is assumed to be a linear relationship through the steps from first to last. I want to make three cautionary comments about this assumption.

First, we need to recognize that the notion of improving students' learning leaves open a wide range of possible outcomes. There are many ways in which learning can be improved that do not all reduce to making learning more effective or more powerful. Sometimes changing how we teach or assess students is designed to achieve different learning outcomes from those previously being aimed for. For example, it might be that the teacher wants to have students who are more politically engaged, or more self-critical, or more self-confident, or more engaged with the subject matter, or the teacher wants to develop skills that can be more directly applied to a professional work situation. The notion of improvement is multidimensional and relative to the intended goals of the teacher-investigator. Improvement cannot and should not be limited to a linear relationship between a prior and later state on a single continuum (D'Andrea and Gosling, 2005).

Second, when evaluating the impact of a change to teaching practice, it is impossible to hold all variables equal. In practice we often make several changes to a course and how it is taught at the same time. We do what we call fine-tuning. Furthermore, other factors outside the tutor's control can have an effect that may support the desired change in student learning or work against it. This means that we must always be cautious when claiming that a particular change has had a particular impact. Ultimately, we have to make professional judgments, within parameters of uncertainty that are typical of complex social situations, about the relationship between a change in teaching and the changes in students that we think are improvements.

Third, pedagogic inquiry should not always be conceptualized as a matter of fixing a problem. Teachers must go through several stages in their thinking and their planning before there is any direct impact on student learning. For example, the first stage may be about encouraging teachers to be more curious about problems in their teaching, or to clarify their understanding, or to discuss alternative goals within a course or program. This stage has two implications for the relationship between inquiry and improved practice. First, pedagogic inquiry may have as its principal purpose to clarify or develop thinking about teaching and its goals and values. Second, investigators may be as interested in assessing or evaluating changes to teachers' thinking or behavior as to students' learning. Investigating how teachers talk to each other, or how their thinking may be changing, or how their confidence to introduce innovations may be increased are all important subjects of inquiry but are not necessarily immediately related to changes to student learning.

With these preliminary thoughts in mind, let us now consider the following question: In what ways would teachers who inquire into their teaching be likely to be better teachers? A second, but closely related, question is, In what ways would institutions that encourage teachers to investigate their practice be likely to be better institutions? I want to answer these questions in two broad ways. The first is about the ways in which investigating teaching affects how teachers think about their teaching and the second is about how their teaching can be better informed.

Teachers who investigate their teaching necessarily have to consider which issues are appropriate subjects for investigation. They have to consider what it is they want to achieve through the investigation, what are the relevant factors in the existing state of affairs, and how well these factors are understood or known. They may also need to consider how they are going to make changes to their practice, how these changes are to be evaluated, and how their effects can be understood. It follows that, by engaging in the process of inquiry, teachers are required to be thoughtful, deliberative, and questioning of their teaching practice and their impact on students. Inquiry therefore encourages curiosity about teaching. It encourages teachers to question and to adopt a critical attitude to taken-for-granted practices and assumptions. Part of the object, as Bass (1999) has suggested, is to acknowledge that teaching problems have the same intellectual validity as research problems.

Through collaborative group discussion of the research questions, the issues tackled can be further expanded to include the ethical basis of teaching (D'Andrea and Gosling, 2005) to create what has been called an "engaged pedagogy" (Kreber, 2005) and a "critical professionalism" (Barnett, 1997). In this way, institutions in which pedagogic inquiry is encouraged benefit from teachers whose interest and enthusiasm in teaching can be regenerated through enhanced intellectual curiosity about pedagogy, collaboration between individual academics, and a healthy debate about the values of the higher education enterprise.

Furthermore, it is through this kind of debate that practices that have been taken for granted as being fit for purpose are called into question. Without an awareness of possible deficiencies or ways in which current practice needs to be brought under critical scrutiny, the scope for improvement in practice is restricted to minor changes to traditional methods. A good example of this review is the way in which assessment practices have been called into question in recent years. In one British university where there has been a significant attempt to reconsider assessment practices, a series of practitioner-led inquiries has been conducted to understand better the processes by which academics come to know about assessment standards (Price and Rust, 1999; Price, 2005; Rust, O'Donovan, and Price, 2005). Pedagogic inquiry in this example has explored and recorded the staff experience of setting standards and using assessment criteria. The aim has certainly been to improve assessment practices, but it has been an essential prerequisite and precondition of achieving any improvements to gain a better understanding of what is actually happening at the present time and raise questions about the effectiveness of current practice. In other words, such inquiries in themselves do not necessarily lead to improved practice, but they lay the ground for a more sustained and better-informed development program.

We can see here how inquiry that seeks to question and raise debate about a practice also requires teachers to become better informed about the context in which the practice occurs. In order for there to be improvement, it is essential that teachers understand more about the context within which they are working. An example, with which I was personally associated, related to a large multicultural university, where a number of claims were being made about the attitude of students toward the curriculum. It was said, for example, that minority students believed the curriculum to be Eurocentric. An inquiry (Jiwani and Gosling, 1997) showed that the picture was much more complex and that attitudes varied between different minority groups, between younger and more mature students, and between males and females. The removal of false certainties was an essential first step toward negotiating changes to the curriculum.

Similar studies have been conducted to better understand class differences and their impact on admissions to university and retention of students (see Johnston, 1999, 2001; Archer and Leathwood, 2003). A recent study undertaken by the Open University demonstrated how early tutor intervention with weak students improved retention (Gibbs, Regan, and Simpson, forthcoming). There are numerous examples of this kind, where the role of pedagogic inquiry, whether conducted by researchers or practitioners, is to provide better data that inform changes in practice.

Inquiry can work in another way to better inform teachers. In the model of action learning considered earlier (McNiff, 1993), inquiry operates as a form of hypothesis testing. An issue or problem is identified within the complex social reality that is the context and practice of the teacher. The teacher develops a hypothesis about a potential solution to the problem. The hypothesis is then tested by doing X; that is, by changing some aspect of the teaching practice within the context in which the identified problem arises. Some form of test or observation is then undertaken to determine whether the problem is solved or alleviated to any or some degree.

Investigation, by providing additional data and by raising new questions, helps to transform intuitive reflection, or what Schön (1987) calls "knowledge-in-action" that is characterized as being "spontaneously delivered without conscious deliberation" (p. 28) into what Eraut describes as "deliberative analysis" (Eraut, 1994). The latter is less common than the routinized knowledge-in-action but becomes essential once the professional is outside the "boundaries of what we have learned to treat as normal" (Schön, 1987, p. 28). Indeed, it is necessary to challenge and be critical of what is called normal if we are to make improvements.

Nine case studies where practitioners challenged and transformed their practice within higher education, and where "research was an everyday activity undertaken by the lecturers in order to understand what was going on in their courses and to learn how to make them work better" are described in Gibbs (1992, p. 21). For example, in that volume, Davies (1992) describes a range of innovations within a graphics design course that he had introduced with two aims: to increase student independence and to increase group effectiveness. The investigation that was undertaken involved using the Approaches to Studying questionnaire and in-depth interviews with students. (The Approaches to Studying questionnaire distinguishes two main approaches to learning: a surface approach and a deep approach. Several versions of the instrument exist. The foundation of this work was laid by Martin and Saljo, 1976, and developed by Entwistle, 1981; Biggs, 1987; and Ramsden, 1992.) Davies's conclusion is that "the range of steps taken to foster a deep approach appear to have been particularly successful" (Davies, 1992, p. 86).

However, this example raises some interesting issues about the status of the knowledge acquired through practitioner-led inquiry. As Davies himself says, there are a number of reasons for having limited confidence in the conclusion he himself draws. There was no control group, and the data cited compare two different student groups. Moreover, the Approaches to Studying questionnaire was "not a suitable device," according to Davies (p. 78), and "as the innovations were introduced gradually there was no opportunity for clear before and after comparisons" (p. 78).

These kinds of limitations to classroom research are not atypical. It is in the nature of this kind of inquiry that it is rarely possible to control variables, use control groups, get clear measures, or have a large enough sample to draw general conclusions. These limitations mean that even if there is a measurable improvement, it is not always possible to be completely confident that it is the result of the change made. Furthermore, the researcher has a strong interest in the success of the inquiry and is therefore not an impartial investigator; moreover, the conclusions are highly context-bound. It is for these kinds of reasons that Gibbs (1992) suggests that the case studies "are offered not as contributions to the research literature on student learning but as resources for lecturers wishing to understand how to improve student learning on their courses" (p. 23).

The assumption here is that although the conditions under which the investigations were undertaken are not sufficiently rigorous to warrant publication as research, they can contribute something to our understanding. This assumption underpins the practice of action research. But if the conclusions are not robust enough to be reported through normal academic channels, why should any reader place any confidence in them and how can they contribute to our understanding?

Murphy (2003) makes similar points about nationally funded (in the United Kingdom) development projects. Although such projects typically incorporate evaluation activity as part of the testing of the ideas being trialed, "HE development projects are by their very nature not designed along the lines of rigorous research studies intended to uncover new knowledge and bring forward convincing evidence to support new claims" (p. 63).

The added difficulty here is the assumption that such projects will uncover and develop best practice that, once identified, can be disseminated to others. But the idea that it is possible to transfer conclusions drawn from experience in one context to the whole HE sector is, as Murphy shows, at best naïve and at worst misleading.

In response to these arguments that the knowledge acquired through development projects or action research is unreliable, it has been said that the purpose of such practitioner-led inquiries is not the production of new knowledge (which is what Boyer, 1990, terms the role of "the scholarship of discovery"). Rather, they are designed to improve practice (Robson, 1993). Their justification is in the context-specific, enhanced interactions between teachers and learners. But this distinction between acquiring new knowledge and improving practice is false. An improved practice must be based on some knowledge claims, however tentative they may be, or else the whole process becomes entirely mystical or puzzling.

These kinds of points have often been made against the action-research model (see, for example, Atkinson and Delamont, 1985), but the conclusion I draw is not that this kind of context-bound inquiry (case study approach) cannot have a role in enhancing practice, but that we need to look for a different account of its role. One suggestion is that there are different kinds of knowledge—personal, local, and public—which relate to the level of the investigation.

Ashwin and Trigwell (2004, p. 121) make the following distinctions:

1. An investigation to inform oneself . . . will result in the production of personal knowledge.
2. An investigation to inform a group within one or more shared contexts . . . will result in the production of local knowledge.
3. An investigation to inform a wider audience . . . will result in the production of public knowledge.

The fundamental idea here is that as the intended audience for the investigation widens, the responsibility increases on the investigator to provide forms of verification that will satisfy or inform the requirements of the wider groups. In local and public knowledge, the investigator will need to satisfy others of the validity of their conclusions, whereas for personal knowledge, varieties of reflection on practice (for example, individual reflection on group discussion or reflective journals and diary notes) are sufficient. But although the conditions to satisfy the requirements of public knowledge may be more stringent (or more narrowly defined) than those that I set for myself, this is not necessarily so. I may set higher standards of verification for myself than those required by public knowledge. In this situation I remain unconvinced that something is reliable knowledge even though it is publicly accepted as such.

We need to combine a number of the points we have considered above to create a multidimensional picture of the salient characteristics of this form of practitioner-led inquiry. These have been called "dimensions of inquiry" (Gordon, D'Andrea, Gosling, and Stefani, 2003; D'Andrea and Gosling, 2005). These are laid out schematically in Table 10.1.

These dimensions of teacher-led inquiry (in comparison with formal educational research) mean that often the conclusions have more limited generalizability, and lower levels of confidence can be placed in the conclusions drawn. But these are not necessarily limitations within the context of the purpose of teacher-led inquiry. When, for example, the attitudes of students toward an innovation is being researched within the restricted sample of a particular cohort of students, then adequate and valid knowledge can be obtained about that group. The fact that it is not possible to generalize from this sample, taken in a time-limited and institutional-specific

### Table 10.1. Dimensions of Inquiry.

| Dimension | Teacher-Led Pedagogic Inquiry |
|---|---|
| Intention | To understand and improve local practice |
| Methodology | Ranges from informal to rigorous |
| Context | Context-specific |
| Focus | Teacher's own practice or that of his or her department or institution |
| Audience | Principally one's own colleagues, potentially the wider community of scholars |
| Level of theory | Often, but not necessarily, limited theorization |
| Discipline | Normally within a discipline context |

context, to students in general is not a limitation because the aim is not to make such generalized claims.

Nevertheless, as Shulman (1993) has argued, it is important that this kind of inquiry becomes to some extent public property so that there is something "shared, discussed, critiqued, exchanged, built upon" (p. 6). In this way, improvements occur because ideas and practices developed by individuals can be tested and critiqued in the open forum of public debate. Furthermore, there can be some accumulation of knowledge and conceptualizations because "It then becomes community property, available for others to build upon" (Shulman, 2000, p. 40).

If we return to our original question whether pedagogic inquiry produces better teachers and better student learning, we must answer, It depends! A teacher who works with reflection-in-action, as Schön (1987) describes it, can be responsive to many professional situations and perform as an outstanding teacher. Teachers who investigate pedagogic practice develop skills in deliberative action, which enables better understanding and better consideration of policy decisions. But that is not to say they can do without the intuitive skills that the teacher needs to respond to the constantly changing nuances of behavior within the classroom. A teacher who has poorly developed skills in the routinized workaday life of the professional will not be transformed by pedagogic investigation alone. For this reason, someone can be a good pedagogic researcher but a limited teacher.

It does not follow from this, however, that pedagogic inquiry has no relationship with improved practice. As we have seen, inquiry encourages teachers to be curious about teaching and learning. It encourages an engaged pedagogy, in which the taken for granted is questioned. It enables teachers to be better informed about the context within which they are working and the impact of the changes they make to their practice. Perhaps most important, it generates debate and discussion about what constitutes improvement in learning.

# References

Archer, L., and Leathwood, C. "Identities, Inequalities and Higher Education." In L. Archer, M. Hutchings, and A. Ross (eds.), *Higher Education and Social Class.* London: Routledge Falmer, 2003.

Ashwin, P., and Trigwell, K. "Investigating Staff and Educational Development." In D. Baume and P. Kahn (eds.), *Enhancing Staff and Educational Development.* London: Routledge Falmer, 2004.

Atkinson, P., and Delamont, S. "Bread and Dreams or Bread and Circuses? A Critique of 'Case Study' Research in Education." In M. Shipman (ed.), *Educational Research: Principles, Policies and Practices.* London: Routledge Falmer, 1985.

Barnett, R. *Higher Education: A Critical Business.* Maidenhead, United Kingdom: Society for Research into Higher Education and Open University, 1997.

Bass, R. "The Scholarship of Teaching: What's the Problem?" *Inventio,* 1999, *1*(1), 1–9.

Biggs, J. *Student Approaches to Learning and Studying.* Hawthorn, Victoria: Australian Council for Educational Research, 1987.

Boyer, E. *Scholarship Reconsidered: Priorities of the Professoriate.* Stanford, Calif.: Carnegie Foundation for the Advancement of Teaching, 1990.

D'Andrea, V-m., and Gosling, D. *Improving Teaching and Learning in Higher Education: A Whole Institution Approach.* Maidenhead, United Kingdom: Open University Press, 2005.

Davies, A. "Encouraging Reflection and Independence on a Graphic Information Design Course." In G. Gibbs (ed.), *Improving the Quality of Student Learning.* Bristol, United Kingdom: Technical and Education Services, 1992.

DeZure, D. (ed.). *Learning from Change.* London: Kogan Page, 2000.

Entwistle, N. *Styles of Learning and Teaching: An Integrated Outline of Educational Psychology for Students, Teachers and Lecturers.* Hoboken, N.J.: Wiley, 1981.

Eraut, M. *Developing Professional Knowledge and Competence.* London: Routledge Falmer, 1994.

Gibbs, G. *Improving the Quality of Student Learning.* Bristol, United Kingdom: Technical and Educational Services, 1992.

Gibbs, G., Regan, P., and Simpson, O. "Improving Student Retention Through Evidence Based Proactive Systems at the Open University (UK)." *Journal of College Retention,* forthcoming.

Gordon, G., D'Andrea, V-m., Gosling, D., and Stefani, L. *Building Capacity for Change in Higher Education: Research on the Scholarship of Teaching.* Bristol: Higher Education Funding Council for England, 2003.

Hargreaves, D. H. *Teaching as a Research-based Profession: Possibilities and Prospects.* London: Teacher Training Agency, 1996.

Hillage, J., Pearson, R., Erson, A., and Tamkin, P. *Excellence in Research on Schools.* London: DfEE, 1998.

Hutchings, P., and Shulman, L. "The Scholarship of Teaching: New Elaborations, New Developments." In D. DeZure (ed.), *Learning from Change.* London: Kogan Page, 2000.

Jiwani, A., and Gosling, D. "Course Design for Multi-Ethnic Student Groups." In C. Rust and G. Gibbs (eds.), *Curriculum Design for Improving Student Learning.* Oxford: Brookes University, 1997.

Johnston, V. "An Analysis of Factors Influencing Undergraduate Progression in the First Year, in a Scottish New University." Paper presented at the International Conference for the First Year Student Experience, Edinburgh, Scotland, 1999.

Johnston, V. "Developing Strategies to Improve Student Retention: Reflections from the Work of Napier University's Student Retention Project." Paper presented to the Society for Research into Higher Education Conference, Cambridge, Dec. 2001.

Kreber, C. "Charting a Critical Course on the Scholarship of University Teaching Movement." *Studies in Higher Education,* 2005, *30*(4), 389–405.

Martin, F., and Saljo, R. "On Qualitative Differences in Learning—1: Outcome and Process." *British Journal of Educational Psychology,* 1976, *46,* 4–11.

McNiff, J. *Teaching as Learning—An Action Research Approach.* London: Routledge, 1993.

Murphy, R. "The Use of Research and Development Projects in Higher Education." In H. Eggins and R. Macdonald (eds.), *The Scholarship of Academic Development.* Buckingham: Society for Research into Higher Education/Open University Press, 2003.

Price, M. "Assessment Standards: The Role of Communities of Practice and the Scholarship of Assessment." *Assessment and Evaluation in Higher Education,* 2005, *30*(3), 215–230.

Price, M., and Rust, C. "The Experience of Introducing a Common Criteria Grid Across an Academic Department." *Quality in Higher Education,* 1999, *5*(2), 133–144.

Ramsden, P. *Learning to Teach in Higher Education.* London: Routledge Falmer, 1992.

Robson, C. *Real World Research.* London: Blackwell, 1993.

Rust, C., O'Donovan, B., and Price, M. "A Social Constructivist Assessment Process Model: How Research Literature Shows Us This Could Be Best Practice." *Assessment and Evaluation in Higher Education,* 2005, *30*(3), 231–240.

Schön, D. *Educating the Reflective Practitioner: How Professionals Think in Action.* London: Temple Smith, 1983.

Schön, D. *Educating the Reflective Practitioner: Towards a New Design for Teaching and Learning in the Professions.* San Francisco: Jossey-Bass, 1987.

Schön, D. "The New Scholarship Requires a New Epistemology: Knowing-in-Action." In D. DeZure (ed.), *Learning from Change: Landmarks in Teaching and Learning in Higher Education from Change Magazine, 1969–1999.* London: Kogan Page, 2000.

Shulman, L. "Teaching as Community Property." *Change,* 1993, *25*(6), 6–7.

Theall, M., and Centra, J. A. "Assessing the Scholarship of Teaching: Valid Decisions." In C. Kreber (ed.), *Scholarship Revisited: Perspectives on the Scholarship of Teaching.* San Francisco: Jossey-Bass, 2001.

Trigwell, K., and Shale, S. "Student Learning and the Scholarship of University Teaching." *Studies in Higher Education,* 2004, *29*(4), 523–536.

Zuber-Skerritt, O. *Action Research in Higher Education.* London: Kogan Page, 1992.

*DAVID GOSLING is an independent higher education consultant and visiting research fellow at the University of Plymouth.*

# 11

*Research-based teaching, understood as student-focused, inquiry-based learning on the one hand and pedagogical inquiry by teachers on the other, holds the greatest promise of success if encouraged at the departmental level, where intended student learning outcomes can be specified for each program and learning experiences designed accordingly.*

# Research-Based Teaching in Relation to Academic Practice: Some Insights Resulting from Previous Chapters

*Carolin Kreber*

The previous chapters discussed the notion of research-based teaching from two broad perspectives and explored some of the issues that are critical to each. In recent years, colleagues have suggested that it would be helpful to keep different perspectives or conceptions separate and use a terminology that deliberately distinguishes, for example, between research-based teaching and research-informed teaching, whereby the former would refer to student-focused, inquiry-based learning (Healey, 2005) and the latter to teaching that is informed by pedagogical research. Usually, two further terms are used in the literature: research-led teaching, where the emphasis in the curriculum lies with the subject content that is taught, and research-oriented, where the emphasis in the curriculum lies with orienting students toward the process of knowledge construction or doing research. (The difference between research-based and research-oriented teaching, as Healey, 2005, suggests, is that the former approach is student-focused whereas the latter is teacher-focused.) As the chapters in this volume by Brew and by Castley show, there are indeed multiple ways in which the relationships between teaching and research can be conceptualized, and many suggestions have been offered in this as well as earlier volumes in terms of how these links could be created or strengthened (see, for example, Jenkins and Healey, 2005).

NEW DIRECTIONS FOR TEACHING AND LEARNING, no. 107, Fall 2006 © Wiley Periodicals, Inc.
Published online in Wiley InterScience (www.interscience.wiley.com) • DOI: 10.1002/tl.249

Elton (as cited in Lueddeke, 2006), suggested that universities today would be well advised to recall von Humboldt's critical insight from almost two hundred years ago regarding the University of Berlin, namely, that universities ought to be places where students and teachers are involved in "a common quest for knowledge" ("Wissenschaft"). It is increasingly recognized that the crucial link between teaching and research lies in the concept of scholarship (Elton, 1992). Elton saw scholarship as the critical interpretation of what is already known, and argued that such interpretation was necessary for both teaching and research (and one may add, learning). Similarly, Andresen (2000) defined scholarship as being characterized by a deep knowledge base, an inquiry orientation, critical reflectivity, and peer review. In his well-known four-faceted conceptualization of scholarship, Boyer (1990) attempted to show the multiple links among the various roles academics perform and to pave the way for a reward system that would more adequately recognize the work associated with each of these roles (particularly teaching).

Academic work, or *academic practice,* as is the preferred term in the United Kingdom, is indeed getting more and more complex as the demands on higher education institutions increase. Among the various challenges already discussed in Chapter One of this volume are the move from elite to mass higher education, changing aspirations in students and evidence that their goals have become increasingly more vocational, a more consumer-oriented student clientele, fewer resources, increased performance accountability in both teaching and research (and more pressures than in the past to demonstrate that research results are useful), and greater expectations of universities to broaden their mandate and to prepare students not only academically but also for their civic, personal, and professional roles in later life. Research-based teaching, as broadly conceptualized in this volume, is one important aspect of academic practice and one way of responding to these challenges. In order to equip students with the skills and knowledge they need in order to be adequately prepared for the demands of later life (for example employability, as discussed in Chapter Five), it has been suggested that higher education institutions provide ample opportunity for students to be involved in inquiry-based learning. Inquiry-based learning, if properly implemented, would serve as a constructive-developmental pedagogy (Baxter Magolda, 1999) aimed at encouraging learners to move from rather naïve to increasingly more sophisticated epistemological belief systems, where knowledge is seen as constructed and the validity of knowledge is recognized as contextual and grounded in the strength or plausibility of arguments (see also Perry, 1970). Baxter Magolda suggests three principles as underlying a constructive developmental pedagogy. These principles include that learners need to be validated for how they know, that their experiences are taken into account when new information is introduced, and that knowledge is constructed together with them (see also Healey, 2005). The three chapters in Part Two of this volume illustrate the forms that such inquiry-based learning may take. However, implementing these suggestions certainly cannot ensure that students actually will have the learning experiences that were intended. Next to knowing that inquiry-based learning is a promising way of supporting students in their learning (for example, the development of thinking processes, problem-solving skills, communication skills, ethical reasoning, and so on), it is also crucially important to know how to best facilitate the process of inquiry-based learning in the various disciplines. Who are our students, how do they learn, what are the challenges of learning in physics compared to learning in English literature, why do students learn the way they do and how can we raise their awareness, self-efficacy, and competence as learners then become key questions to explore. As we have seen in Part Three of this volume, these are obviously the kinds of questions that get addressed when academics engage in the process of inquiry-based learning about teaching, or alternatively, the scholarship of teaching and learning.

In Chapter Seven, Huber suggested that disciplines bring their unique styles to the study of educational phenomena, both in relation to the issues they are prone to address and the methodologies they are likely to use. It seems clear that the greatest advancements in teaching and learning will result from a wide exchange or sharing of these various perspectives across disciplinary boundaries. In Chapter Nine, D'Andrea observed that much pedagogical inquiry lacks a clear theoretical framework within which to situate the research questions and provide a frame of reference for the analysis and interpretation of results. She argued that greater attention should be given to methodological issues so as to render engagement in pedagogical inquiry a more meaningful exercise. It would seem that placing stronger emphasis on how disciplines such as philosophy, sociology, or history (to mention just some obvious examples next to psychology) could uniquely enrich the repertoire of educational research methodologies is indeed warranted.

I argued in Chapter Eight that educational development units (EDUs) have an important role to play in supporting teachers in this important aspect of their work. Not only should EDUs encourage reflection and critical reflection on teaching and assessment methods, student learning, and educational purposes and goals, but they should also introduce both discipline-specific and generic ways of carrying out such work.

In Chapter Ten, Gosling argued that it can be assumed that teaching and learning are positively affected by academic staff engaging in the process of pedagogical inquiry and highlighted the conditions that make this positive link most likely.

At the end of the volume two questions need to be raised: First, should every teacher be involved in inquiry-based learning about teaching, and second, is all teaching that does not directly involve students in inquiry-based learning about the subject problematic? With both questions, the answer ought to be, It depends. Both phenomena are perhaps best understood as being practiced along a continuum. As for inquiry-based learning about teaching, it would be outright foolish to expect every staff member to engage in pedagogical research on teaching and learning and to disseminate the results through conferences or written work. At the same time, academic practice needs to be underpinned by scholarship that is associated with the notion of reflective practice and critical reflectivity. Although all staff surely should not be expected to engage in pedagogical research, all staff can be expected to engage in content, process, and premise reflection on the purposes and goals of their teaching, student learning, and teaching and assessment methods. This reflection would ensure that their teaching is at least "research-informed," which in turn would require adequate preparation of all staff for their teaching roles along the lines discussed in Chapter Eight.

As far as the second question is concerned, one may not want to suggest that any one method of teaching is superior irrespective of the uniqueness of different teaching and learning situations. While lectures may generally be considered to be less effective than more interactive methods in promoting higher-order learning (Garrison and Archer, 2000), it has been argued that they can be used effectively for the purpose of demonstrating higher-order thinking skills (Brookfield, 1991). Furthermore, many courses, particularly in the sciences, are taught not through lectures alone but make use of tutorials or labs. Although the lecture may not involve students in inquiry-based learning per se, the tutorials and the work they are expected to complete by the end of the semester may be firmly based on such an approach. The pedagogical principles underlying inquiry-based learning, so it would seem, can be implemented or practiced not only to varying degrees but also in a variety of ways and may not be bound to any one method. However, it is also clear that some methods or approaches are better suited than others for helping students develop the thinking and research skills needed for both understanding the discipline and succeeding in later life. Although a lecture that is purely noninteractive (as in a physics teacher spending the entire fifty minutes of class time talking nonstop about how certain formulas provide certain solutions, possibly supported by visual aids such as carefully designed PowerPoint slides, handouts, and the chalkboard, as well as the student workbook containing the exact same examples, not asking a single question of students) may not cause any harm and may help some students to understand the material even better, it is questionable whether such pedagogical practice contributes anything by way of fostering student self-direction in learning or higher-order thinking skills, let alone an appreciation of how the subject links up with broader ethical, environmental, or societal concerns. Granted, to a large extent all this depends on what is being said in those fifty minutes, and how. Maybe a teacher as described above who in addition keeps eye contact with students and appears to be relatively motivated and well prepared has some positive influence on students even though he or she does not involve students in the process of knowledge construction. Perhaps such a teacher is even described as a great teacher by some colleagues or even as an enthusiastic teacher by others (clearly, what such descriptors or reputations really involve is always a function of the standard and culture of teaching practice at the institution concerned). Yet even in physics one can easily imagine a more interactive lecture in which teachers, during their lecturing, practice the principles of a constructive-developmental pedagogy. At the most basic level this approach would involve asking questions to elicit students' present ways of thinking about and understanding the problem and together with them exploring alternatives.

However, the larger problem is that the actual learning outcomes achieved by students by the time they graduate may be less a function of individual teachers' approaches to teaching (though these do matter!) than a consequence of the structure and pedagogical orientation of the program or curriculum they studied. Involving students in inquiry-based learning about teaching, therefore, has to be a departmental rather than purely an individual effort, as it is at the departmental level that it is decided what experiences students in different programs will or should have. While it is indeed important how individual staff members teach and what their educational goals and purposes are, it is obvious that the student experience can be understood and influenced most strongly only at the program level, where intended learning outcomes are specified and opportunities for inquiry-based learning can be optimized through collaborative program planning. This preference means, in turn, that all staff teaching on the program (whether they primarily give lectures or facilitate tutorials) would need to engage regularly in content, process, and premise reflection on teaching and reach their decisions dialogically. Indeed, initiatives aimed at introducing staff to inquiry-based learning about teaching (see Chapter Eight) may have the greatest prospects of success when aimed directly at groups of staff working jointly on the design or redesign of particular programs.

Within each such program team, team members may place the focus of their academic practice very differently. Some may wish to engage in full-blown pedagogical research, while others may see their role as making sure that the results of that research are used during program design so that it is research-informed; still others may wish to serve primarily as content specialists who ensure that the teaching is research-led and the subject matter up to date.

## References

Andresen, L. W. "A Usable, Trans-Disciplinary Conception of Scholarship." *Higher Education Research and Development,* 2000, *19*(2), 137–153.

Baxter Magolda, M. *Creating Contexts for Learning and Self-Authorship: Constructive-Developmental Pedagogy.* Nashville, Tenn.: Vanderbilt University Press, 1999.

Boyer, E. *Scholarship Reconsidered.* Stanford, Calif.: Carnegie Foundation for the Advancement of Teaching, 1990.

Brookfield, S. *The Skillful Teacher.* San Francisco: Jossey-Bass, 1991.

Elton, L. "Research, Teaching and Scholarship in an Expanding Higher Education System." *Higher Education Quarterly,* 1992, *46*(3), 252–268.

Garrison, D. R., and Archer, W. *A Transactional Perspective on Teaching-Learning: A Framework for Adult and Higher Education.* Oxford: Pergamon, 2000.

Healey, M. "Linking Research and Teaching: Exploring Disciplinary Spaces and the Role of Inquiry-Based Learning." In R. Barnett (ed.), *Reshaping the University: New Relationships Between Research, Scholarship and Teaching*. Maidenhead, United Kingdom: Open University Press, 2005.

Jenkins, A., and Healey, M. *Institutional Strategies to Link Teaching and Research*. York: Higher Education Academy, 2005. http://www.heacademy.ac.uk/resources.asp?process=full_record&section=generic&id=585. Accessed Aug. 2, 2006.

Lueddeke, G. "Reconciling Research and Teaching in Higher Education: An Examination of Disciplinary Variation, the Curriculum and Learning." Discussion paper 3. School of Medicine, Southhampton Institute, United Kingdom, 2006.

Perry, W. G. *Forms of Intellectual and Ethical Development in the College Years: A Scheme.* New York: Rinehart and Winston, 1970.

CAROLIN KREBER *is director of the Centre for Teaching, Learning and Assessment at the University of Edinburgh, where she is also professor of teaching and learning in higher education in the Department of Higher and Community Education.*

# INDEX

# Back Issue/Subscription Order Form

Copy or detach and send to:
**Jossey-Bass, A Wiley Imprint, 989 Market Street, San Francisco CA 94103-1741**

**Call or fax toll-free: Phone 888-378-2537 6:30AM – 3PM PST; Fax 888-481-2665**

Back Issues: Please send me the following issues at $29 each
(Important: please include ISBN number for each single issue you order.)

_____

_____

_____

$ _____ Total for single issues

$ _____ SHIPPING CHARGES: SURFACE     Domestic Canadian
                                First Item     $5.00     $6.00
                                Each Add'l Item  $3.00     $1.50
              For next-day and second-day delivery rates, call the number listed above.

Subscriptions   Please __ start __ renew my subscription to *New Directions for Teaching and Learning* for the year 2__ at the following rate:

| U.S. | __ Individual $80 | __ Institutional $195 |
| Canada | __ Individual $80 | __ Institutional $235 |
| All Others | __ Individual $104 | __ Institutional $269 |

Online subscriptions available too!
**For more information about online subscriptions visit
www.interscience.wiley.com**

$ _____ Total single issues and subscriptions (Add appropriate sales tax for your state for single issue orders. No sales tax for U.S. subscriptions. Canadian residents, add GST for subscriptions and single issues.)

__Payment enclosed (U.S. check or money order only)
__VISA __ MC __ AmEx #_____ Exp. Date _____

Signature _____ Day Phone _____
__ Bill me (U.S. institutional orders only. Purchase order required.)

Purchase order # _____
                  **Federal Tax ID13559302**                **GST 89102 8052**

Name _____

Address _____

_____

Phone _____ E-mail _____

For more information about Jossey-Bass, visit our Web site at **www.josseybass.com**

**TL101    Enhancing Learning with Laptops in the Classroom**
*Linda B. Nilson, Barbara E. Weaver*
This volume contains case studies—mostly from Clemson University's leading-edge laptop program—that address victories as well as glitches in teaching with laptop computers in the classroom. Disciplines using laptops include psychology, music, statistics, animal sciences, and humanities. The volume also advises faculty on making a laptop mandate successful at their university, with practical guidance for both pedagogy and student learning.
ISBN: 0-7879-8049-8

**TL100    Alternative Strategies for Evaluating Student Learning**
*Michelle V. Achacoso, Marilla D. Svinicki*
Teaching methods are adapting to the modern era, but innovation in assessment of student learning lags behind. This volume examines theory and practical examples of creative new methods of evaluation, including authentic testing, testing with multimedia, portfolios, group exams, visual synthesis, and performance-based testing. Also investigates improving students' ability to take and learn from tests, before and after.
ISBN: 0-7879-7970-8

**TL99    Addressing Faculty and Student Classroom Improprieties**
*John M. Braxton, Alan E. Bayer*
Covers the results of a large research study on occurrence and perceptions of classroom improprieties by both students and faculty. When classroom norms are violated, all parties in a classroom are affected, and teaching and learning suffer. The authors offer guidelines for both student and faculty classroom behavior and how institutions might implement those suggestions.
ISBN: 0-7879-7794-2

**TL98    Decoding the Disciplines: Helping Students Learn Disciplinary Ways of Thinking**
*David Pace, Joan Middendorf*
The Decoding the Disciplines model is a way to teach students the critical-thinking skills required to understand their specific discipline. Faculty define bottlenecks to learning, dissect the ways experts deal with the problematic issues, and invent ways to model experts' thinking for students. Chapters are written by faculty in diverse fields who successfully used these methods and became involved in the scholarship of teaching and learning.
ISBN: 0-7879-7789-6

**TL97    Building Faculty Learning Communities**
*Milton D. Cox, Laurie Richlin*
A very effective way to address institutional challenges is a faculty learning community. FLCs are useful for preparing future faculty, reinvigorating senior faculty, and implementing new courses, curricula, or campus initiatives. The results of FLCs parallel those of student learning communities, such as retention, deeper learning, respect for others, and greater civic participation. This volume describes FLCs from a practitioner's perspective, with plenty of advice, wisdom, and lessons for starting your own FLC.
ISBN: 0-7879-7568-0

**TL96    Online Student Ratings of Instruction**
*Trav D. Johnson, D. Lynn Sorenson*
Many institutions are adopting Web-based student ratings of instruction, or are considering doing it, because online systems have the potential to save

time and money among other benefits. But they also present a number of challenges. The authors of this volume have firsthand experience with electronic ratings of instruction. They identify the advantages, consider costs and benefits, explain their solutions, and provide recommendations on how to facilitate online ratings.
ISBN: 0-7879-7262-2

TL95    **Problem-Based Learning in the Information Age**
*Dave S. Knowlton, David C. Sharp*
Provides information about theories and practices associated with problem-based learning, a pedagogy that allows students to become more engaged in their own education by actively interpreting information. Today's professors are adopting problem-based learning across all disciplines to faciliate a broader, modern definition of what it means to learn. Authors provide practical experience about designing useful problems, creating conducive learning environments, facilitating students' activities, and assessing students' efforts at problem solving.
ISBN: 0-7879-7172-3

TL94    **Technology: Taking the Distance out of Learning**
*Margit Misangyi Watts*
This volume addresses the possibilities and challenges of computer technology in higher education. The contributors examine the pressures to use technology, the reasons not to, the benefits of it, the feeling of being a learner as well as a teacher, the role of distance education, and the place of computers in the modern world. Rather than discussing only specific successes or failures, this issue addresses computers as a new cultural symbol and begins meaningful conversations about technology in general and how it affects education in particular.
ISBN: 0-7879-6989-3

TL93    **Valuing and Supporting Undergraduate Research**
*Joyce Kinkead*
The authors gathered in this volume share a deep belief in the value of undergraduate research. Research helps students develop skills in problem solving, critical thinking, and communication, and undergraduate researchers' work can contribute to an institution's quest to further knowledge and help meet societal challenges. Chapters provide an overview of undergraduate research, explore programs at different types of institutions, and offer suggestions on how faculty members can find ways to work with undergraduate researchers.
ISBN: 0-7879-6907-9

TL92    **The Importance of Physical Space in Creating Supportive Learning Environments**
*Nancy Van Note Chism, Deborah J. Bickford*
The lack of extensive dialogue on the importance of learning spaces in higher education environments prompted the essays in this volume. Chapter authors look at the topic of learning spaces from a variety of perspectives, elaborating on the relationship between physical space and learning, arguing for an expanded notion of the concept of learning spaces and furnishings, talking about the context within which decision making for learning spaces takes place, and discussing promising approaches to the renovation of old learning spaces and the construction of new ones.
ISBN: 0-7879-6344-5

TL91    **Assessment Strategies for the On-Line Class: From Theory to Practice**
*Rebecca S. Anderson, John F. Bauer, Bruce W. Speck*
Addresses the kinds of questions that instructors need to ask themselves as
they begin to move at least part of their students' work to an on-line format.
Presents an initial overview of the need for evaluating students' on-line work
with the same care that instructors give to the work in hard-copy format.
Helps guide instructors who are considering using on-line learning in
conjunction with their regular classes, as well as those interested in going
totally on-line.
ISBN: 0-7879-6343-7

TL90    **Scholarship in the Postmodern Era: New Venues, New Values, New
Visions**
*Kenneth J. Zahorski*
A little over a decade ago, Ernest Boyer's *Scholarship Reconsidered* burst upon
the academic scene, igniting a robust national conversation that maintains
its vitality to this day. This volume aims at advancing that important
conversation. Its first section focuses on the new settings and circumstances
in which the act of scholarship is being played out; its second identifies and
explores the fresh set of values currently informing today's scholarly
practices; and its third looks to the future of scholarship, identifying trends,
causative factors, and potentialities that promise to shape scholars and their
scholarship in the new millennium.
ISBN: 0-7879-6293-7

TL89    **Applying the Science of Learning to University Teaching and Beyond**
*Diane F. Halpern, Milton D. Hakel*
Seeks to build on empirically validated learning activities to enhance what and
how much is learned and how well and how long it is remembered. Demonstrates that the movement for a real science of learning—the application of
scientific principles to the study of learning—has taken hold both under the
controlled conditions of the laboratory and in the messy real-world settings
where most of us go about the business of teaching and learning.
ISBN: 0-7879-5791-7

TL88    **Fresh Approaches to the Evaluation of Teaching**
*Christopher Knapper, Patricia Cranton*
Describes a number of alternative approaches, including interpretive and
critical evaluation, use of teaching portfolios and teaching awards,
performance indicators and learning outcomes, technology-mediated
evaluation systems, and the role of teacher accreditation and teaching
scholarship in instructional evaluation.
ISBN: 0-7879-5789-5

TL87    **Techniques and Strategies for Interpreting Student Evaluations**
*Karron G. Lewis*
Focuses on all phases of the student rating process—from data-gathering
methods to presentation of results. Topics include methods of encouraging
meaningful evaluations, mid-semester feedback, uses of quality teams and
focus groups, and creating questions that target individual faculty needs and
interest.
ISBN: 0-7879-5789-5